The Yorkshire Terrier Handbook

Handbook

D. Caroline Coile, Ph.D.

With Full-color Photographs
Drawings by Michele Earle-Bridges

BARRON'S

Acknowledgments

Many Yorkshire Terrier owners supplied information for this book, foremost among them Carolyn Hensley, to whom I am profoundly grateful for her endlessly patient explanations of all things Yorkie and her chapter-by-chapter critiques of the manuscript. Another special thanks is due Rae Tanner, who provided invaluable information and critiques on the Yorkie in performance sports, to Cindy Najera for information from a professional groomer's point of view, and to Dr. Carla Mayer for checking the veterinary information. As always, the folks at Barron's double-checked, tweaked, and somehow made the whole thing into a book under the guidance of editor extraordinaire, Seymour Weiss.

About the Author

Caroline Coile is an award-winning author who has written numerous articles about dogs for both scientific and lay publications. Her writing credits also include many well-respected books on the various aspects of dogs and dog sports. She holds a Ph.D. in neuroscience and behavior with special interests in canine sensory systems, genetics and behavior. An active dog fancier since 1963, her own dogs have been nationally ranked in confomation, obedience and performance activities.

All inquiries should be addressed to:
Barron's Educational Series, Inc.
250 Wireless Boulevard
Hauppauge, New York 11788
http://www.barronseduc.com

International Standard Book No. 0-7641-2585-0
Library of Congress Catalog Card No. 2003056063

Library of Congress Cataloging-in-Publication Data
Coile, D. Caroline.
    The Yorkshire terrier handbook / D. Caroline Coile ; drawings by Michele Earle-Bridges.
        p. cm.
    Includes bibliographical references (p.).
    ISBN 0-7641-2585-0
    1. Yorkshire terrier. I. Title.

SF429.Y6C65   2003
636.76—dc21   2003056063

Printed in Hong Kong
9 8 7 6 5 4 3 2 1

Cover Photos

All photos by Isabelle Francais with the exception of the two bottom photos on the front cover by Pets by Paulette.

Photo Credits

Barbara Augello: pages 27, 29, 105, 119, 122, 126, 129, 137; Kent and Donna Dannen: pages 2, 9 (top), 16, 33, 43, 46, 55, 60, 66, 80 (bottom), 82, 89, 101, 114, 143; Tara Darling: pages 12, 57, 58, 62, 77, 98, 111, 115, 153; Cheryl A. Ertelt: pages 25 (top), 40, 79, 88, 94, 118, 120; Isabelle Francais: pages vi, 6, 14, 15, 17, 20, 30, 32, 49, 63, 64, 65, 80 (top), 84, 85, 91, 93, 99, 106, 124, 135, 136, 142, 146, 150, 151; Nance Photography: pages 9 (bottom), 24, 28 (top), 59, 125, 130, 133, 138, 140, 149; Pets by Paulette: pages 4, 5, 8, 10, 23, 25 (bottom), 26, 28 (bottom), 31, 35, 37 (top and bottom), 38, 50, 52, 69, 70, 71, 73, 97, 109, 117, 141, 152

Important Note

This pet handbook gives advice to the reader on how to buy or adopt, and care for a Yorkshire Terrier. The author and publisher consider it important to point out that the advice given in this book applies to normally developed puppies or adult dogs, acquired from recognized dog breeders or adoption sources, dogs that have been examined and are in excellent physical health with good temperament.

Anyone who adopts a fully-grown dog should be aware that the animal has already formed its basic impressions of human beings and their customary actions. The new owner should watch the animal carefully, especially its attitude and behavior toward humans. If possible, the new owner should meet the previous owner before adopting the dog. If the dog comes from a shelter, the new owner should make an effort to obtain information about the dog's background, personality, and any individual peculiarities. Dogs coming from abusive homes or from homes in which they have been treated abnormally may react to handling in an unnatural manner, and they may have a tendency to snap or bite. Such dogs should only be adopted by people experienced with handling canine behavior problems.

Caution is further advised in the association of children with dogs, both puppies and adults, and in meeting other dogs, whether on or off lead.

Even well-behaved and carefully supervised dogs sometimes do damage to someone else's property or cause accidents. It is therefore in the owner's interest to be adequately insured against such eventualities, and we strongly urge all dog owners to purchase a liability policy that covers the dog.

Contents

1. In Days of York   1
   Terrier Roots   1
   Flight of Fancy   3
   Yankee Yorkies   5
   Too Much of a Good Thing   5

2. Yorkie Yearnings   7
   The Friend of a Lifetime   7
   The Real Yorkshire Terrier   7
   Size Matters   9
   Meet Your Match   10
   Looking for a Little Love   12
   Puppy Picking   18

3. Your Yorkie Youngster   19
   Welcome Home   19
   Accessorize   20
   A Safe Haven   21
   Raising Havoc   23
   Yorkie Pediatrics   29
   Baby Food   32
   Puppy Grooming   33

4. Brains and Beauty   35
   The Click Is the Trick   37
   Basic Training   39
   Higher Education   42
   School Days   43
   Yorkshire Terrors   43

5. Yorkshire Terrier Nutrition   51
    The Nature of Nutrition   51
    Commercial, Raw, and Home-Prepared Diets   52
    Right on Time   55
    The Porkie Yorkie   56
    The Picky Yorkie   57
    Water   58
    Special Diets   58

6. Crowning Glories   61
    Brushing   62
    Trimming   64
    Bathing   68
    Topknots   71
    Wrapping   75
    Finishing Touches   75
    Professional Groomers   76

7. Good Grooming   78
    Skin Care   78
    External Parasites   79
    Nail Care   81
    Dental Care   82
    Ear Care   84

8. Medical Matters   86
    Give Your Yorkie the Once-Over   86
    Yorkie Signs and Solutions   87
    Small Dog First Aid   102
    Poisoning   106

9. Small Victories   108
    Little Show-Offs   108
    Mind Games   110
    Canine Good Citizens   112
    Leaps and Bounds   115
    Hot on the Trail   117
    Safety First   118
    Fun and Games   118
    Therapy Dogs   121

10.	Breeding Quality	123
	Breeding by the Numbers	123
	Good Homes Come to Good Breeders	124
	The Perfect Match	124
	Breeding and Whelping	126
	Postnatal Care of the Dam	128
	Neonatal Care	130
	Tail Docking and Dewclaw Removal	131
	Growing Up Yorkie	132
11.	Yorkies Through the Years	134
	Aging Gracefully	134
	Senior Health	136
	When You've Done Everything	139
12.	The Yorkshire Terrier Standard of Perfection	144
	Yorkie Resources	147
	Index	151

Chapter One

In Days of York

With aerobatic leaps and precision pounces, he stalks and captures his prey. His family laughs at this show with his toy, but this is serious business to a Yorkshire Terrier. He answers an ancestral call, one compelling him to chase, catch, and shake his imaginary prey. He is terrier to the core.

Terrier Roots

Terrier roots run deep. By 200 B.C. hunters used small dogs called *agassoei* to follow quarry underground. The earliest European skeletal evidence of a terrier-like dog dates from shortly after that time. The Romans called such dogs *terrarii*, from the Latin "terra," for earth. A sixteenth-century description reads:

"Another sorte which hunteth the Foxe and the Badger or Grey onely, whom we call Terrars, because they (after the manner and custom of Ferrets in searching for Connyes) creepe into the grounde, and by that

Yorkshire Terriers began life as rugged vermin hunters.

means make afrayde, nyppe, and byte the Fox and the badger in such sort, that eyther they teare them in peeces with thayre teeth beying in the bosome of the earth, or ese hayle and pull them perforce out of their lurking angles, dark dongeons and close caves" (Johannes Caius, in his *De Canibus Britainicis*, 1576).

Early terriers seldom received the adulation given dogs more often associated with nobility. But terriers played a vital role by ridding farms and homes of vermin and eventually providing sport for commoners.

Terriers flourished in the British Isles, partly because the Forest Laws, some dating to the eleventh century, forbade serfs to own dogs capable of hunting large game. But without dogs, serfs' crops and homes might be overrun with vermin and their kettles meatless. The Forest Laws allowed serfs to own smaller dogs that could pass through a 7-inch hoop. Not just any small dog would serve. It had to be one that could follow and dispatch vermin in tight places and be easily carried for poaching. It had to be quick enough to chase rabbits and

The Yorkshire's ancestors ratted along the many watercourses in the north of England.

tough enough to face rats. That it might also entertain the family, warm a child's bed, or provide bragging rights for its hunting abilities were bonuses that eventually shaped the terrier's future. Puppies from exceptional hunters populated various villages, eventually creating separate strains in different villages.

The Industrial Revolution of the early 1800s further shaped these strains into breeds. Urbanization kindled the need for organized amusement when little entertainment was available to commoners. Affordable entertainment usually involved gambling, especially on animals. Taverns would set up a small pit, fill it with rats, throw in a dog, encourage some wagering, and provide inexpensive entertainment. Owners boasting of their terriers' rat killing prowess could

test their dogs, perhaps winning wagers and cultivating a market for puppies or stud fees. Travelers' accounts of the best dogs they had seen elsewhere enhanced the reputation of certain strains.

One such strain, the Waterside Terrier, was already in the northern England shire of York by the late 1700s. Weighing about 10 pounds and sporting a long or rough, often grayish, coat, the Waterside Terrier excelled at ratting in the pits and along the docks.

Another prominent strain, the Roseneath Terrier, hailed from Roseneath in the Isle of Butte. Weighing between 10 and 16 pounds, and colored fawn or silver gray, the Roseneath Terrier gave rise to the Skye, Paisley, and Clydesdale Terriers. The latter two, sometimes considered the same breed, were small dogs with prick ears and long, straight, silky coats that sometimes trailed the ground. The Paisley was blue and silver, while the Clydesdale was blue and tan. Both breeds vanished by the early 1900s, but not before their genes were incorporated in other strains—including probably the Yorkshire Terrier.

England's Industrial Revolution brought an influx of workers from abroad, including many Scottish weavers who worked in Yorkshire's textile mills. They brought their Paisley, Clydesdale, and old style of Skye terriers with them to help rid the mills of rats. Their Scotch terriers soon interbred with native English Terriers, including the Waterside Terrier. The ingredients needed for the Yorkshire Terrier were there, awaiting a few fortuitous matings.

Those matings involved a crossbred Scotch terrier named Swift's Old Crab, a small dog of about 9 pounds, with a medium length coat and tan points; a Skye or Paisley Terrier named Kershaw's Kitty, a drop eared dog with a long solid blue coat; and an Old English Terrier whose name has been lost but is described as having tan points, with a grayish back coat. These dogs are considered the foundation of the Yorkshire Terrier.

Huddersfield Ben, called by some "the father of the breed."

Flight of Fancy

In the late 1800s the emergence of dog shows propelled many working-class dogs into high society. The first dog show in 1859 was so successful that other shows quickly followed, encouraging the development of judging standards for as many breeds as possible. Queen Victoria's interest in dog shows made owning a purebred dog a status symbol; a pedigreed dog that could also adorn his mistress's lap on a carriage ride became a high-society fashion statement.

The small silky-coated dog in brilliant blue fit the bill as show dog and lady's adornment. Their working-class

breeders quickly turned their talents to producing the most glamorous specimens that would appeal to the new well-paying market.

In 1865 one of the most influential dogs of the fledgling breed was born: Huddersfield Ben. Tightly inbred and a great show dog, Ben was a popular and prepotent sire. Although his life was cut short when he was run over by a carriage in 1871, his influence still survives.

Ben, along with other rough-coated terriers, was exhibited as a Broken Haired Scotch Terrier until 1870, when a reporter suggested that such a fine group of dogs deserved its own name. He suggested they be called Yorkshire Terriers after the area in which they had been most improved. The name, sometimes with variations (such as the Yorkshire Blue and Tan Silky Coated Terrier) caught on, and in 1886 the Kennel Club recognized the Yorkshire Terrier as a separate breed. The first Champion Yorkshire Terrier male recorded was Merry Mentor, and the first Champion female was Ashton Queen, both of which gained their titles in 1897. The first Yorkshire Terrier breed club was formed in 1898.

The Yorkshire Terrier's future would now be shaped by dog shows rather than work. Its patrons cloaked the little rat catcher in the finest coat and placed him on velvet pillows. Never the fool, the Yorkshire Terrier

Small Talk
Yorkie Doodle Dandy

Perhaps the most famous Yorkie in history was a war dog! "Corporal" Smoky was a 4-pound Yorkie found in a jungle foxhole during World War II. She accompanied her adoptive owner on twelve missions in the Pacific, entertained wounded troops with her many tricks, and was voted Best Mascot in the Southwest Pacific. She saved the day when a wire had to be run through an 8-inch culvert under a runway to make an airstrip operational. She traversed the long tunnel, guided by her owner's calls from the opposite end, pulling the wire behind her. After the war she became a television personality. Her exploits are memorialized in the book, *Yorkie Doodle Dandy*.

embraced his newfound life of luxury, but he steadfastly refused to forsake his terrier ways.

Yankee Yorkies

By the 1870s, fancy terriers not only were the vogue in Europe, but were also gracing the finer American parlors. The first recorded birth of an American-born Yorkshire Terrier, a dog named Jack, was in 1872. American dog shows first offered classes specifically for Yorkshire Terriers in 1878, divided into categories of under and over 5 pounds. That same year Yorkshire Terriers were first shown at the Westminster Kennel Club. The thirty-three entries were about equally divided between the two weight divisions. Early Yorkies ranged in size from about 3 to 13 pounds, but during the next two decades size became more uniformly petite.

In 1885, a year after the American Kennel Club (AKC) was established, the Yorkshire Terrier was admitted in the AKC stud book. The year 1890

saw the first American Champion, a great-great-grandson of Huddersfield Ben named Bradford Harry.

The Yorkshire Terrier Association of America formed in 1919, but only lasted about 5 years. The present AKC parent club, the Yorkshire Terrier Club of America (YTCA), was formed in 1954. Yorkshire Terriers were first registered in Canada in 1888 and in Mexico in 1893.

Too Much of a Good Thing

The Yorkshire Terrier remained a favorite of the upper crust's secret treasure for many years, but eventually all secrets get out. Only 173 Yorkies were AKC registered in 1949, but by 1960 more than 1000 were registered, by 1970 more than 13,000, and by 1980 nearly 25,000. In 1995 the Yorkshire Terrier entered the top ten most popular breeds

The Yorkshire Terrier made its American debut during the latter part of the nineteenth century.

5

The Yorkshire Terrier's beauty and personality enabled the breed to quickly evolve into a highly competitive show dog.

with almost 37,000 registrations, peaking with more than 42,000 registrations in 2002. It is presently the sixth most popular breed in America.

The breed saw a similar rise to fame in its homeland of Great Britain. Only 300 Yorkies were registered with the British Kennel Club in 1932; by the 1970s it had become the most popular breed in Britain, with more than 25,000 annual registrations. It remains among the top ten most popular breeds.

Popularity is seldom good for a breed. Not everybody who is drawn to a popular breed has the right motives or background. Some see popular breeds as money-makers, and unfortunate dogs live as caged puppy-producing machines. Others breed their family pet out of naivety, adding to the glutted market. Eventually even the Yorkshire Terrier outgrew the number of good homes available. This once rare dog is now found in shelters and rescue situations. Yorkie lovers are overwhelmed helping Yorkies in need, and dedicated breeders try to maintain a core of healthy Yorkies with correct conformation and temperament, true to their Yorkshire ancestors.

Chapter Two

Yorkie Yearnings

With their tumbleweed look and "pick me" attitude, Yorkshire Terrier puppies are irresistible. Caring for a Yorkie takes time, energy, money, and commitment but returns love, companionship, and entertainment. Yorkies prove you *can* buy love . . . just make sure you get the best love you can buy.

The Friend of a Lifetime

Life with a Yorkie means sharing strolls in the neighborhood, quiet moments at home, or car trips around town. A Yorkie is a pint-size protector, frolicsome friend, and perky partner who makes adventures out of mundane tasks. But life with a Yorkie also means midnight walks in the rain, soiled floors, lost freedom, and countless expenses. Most of all, it means making a commitment that lasts longer than most marriages.

Yorkies make such good companions because they form deep attachments to their families. Their families aren't always so loyal. When the dog loses her novelty or becomes inconvenient, she's exiled to the garage or taken to the animal shelter. Make sure you want a Yorkie for life before inviting one into your family.

The Real Yorkshire Terrier

It's easy to fall in love with the image of the Yorkshire Terrier looking glamorous adorning a pillow or cute poking a curious face from a handbag or frisky with her toys. But there's another side. Yorkies don't look so glamorous covered in mats, cute using your carpets for their toilet, or fun ripping the pages from your favorite book. Yorkies are dogs—not stuffed toys or household ornaments.

The Yorkie's flowing cape is among the most beautiful in the canine world, but it requires dedication to keep it long, clean, and tangle-free. Her coat can be clipped in a pixie coif, but that means visiting

Small Talk
Yorkies Can Be Heros

Spock, a 7-year-old Yorkie, heard his 78-year-old master thumping on the wall after falling and badly breaking his leg. Spock ran upstairs to awaken a family member for help. Daisy, a Yorkie mix who is also a Hearing Dog for the Deaf, alerted her deaf owner to the fire alarm—and the fire that caused it to go off. A Yorkie named Garcia barked frantically to alert his people to the fact that their new puppy had fallen from the dock. The puppy was rescued in the nick of time.

the beauty shop every couple of months, and still doesn't free you of the obligation to keep it clean and brushed.

Those who know the Yorkie know it's not the coat that really sets this

The Yorkshire Terrier presents an elegant image—but she's a real dog that isn't suited for everybody.

dog apart, however. Imbued with a zest for life and all it brings her way, the Yorkie makes every day a party. Part clown, part gracious hostess, she delights in entertaining a party of one or a dozen. She is a natural-born show-off. She will gladly help in dinner preparation from underfoot or in television program selection from your lap. When she is good, she is very, very good . . .

But when she is bad—actually, she's still not terribly bad! She can show her appreciation for your valuables by adding her signature teeth marks. She may start an argument she can't finish with a larger dog, secure in the knowledge you'll whisk her to safety. Her terrier ancestry gives her a sense of adventure and independence, some would say even a stubborn streak. But that has been tempered by generations of selection as a companion, and the Yorkie today is a spicy blend of feisty mischief-maker and devoted companion.

Yorkies and other animals: Terriers are notorious for their scrappiness, but most Yorkies have risen above such petty quarreling. Yorkies of the opposite sex will generally get along well, but even so, minor scrabbles occur. Occasionally two Yorkies of the same sex will develop an intense dislike for one another, to the point that they must be separated to keep the peace. Yorkies can get along well with cats, but they should be supervised around small mammals such as rats and gerbils, which could prove too hard to resist.

Yorkies and children: Yorkies can make fun-loving friends for children, but they can be hurt by rough or careless play. They are not the breed of choice for very young children who may not realize that they are being rough.

Exercise: Just because Yorkies are little doesn't mean they don't need exercise or appreciate adventure. They can get a good workout racing around an apartment and can enjoy stalking and killing toys every bit as much as their ancestors enjoyed hunting rats. They seek out entertainment, learn quickly, and are eager to please as long as there is fun involved.

Yorkies are adventurers at heart.

Size Matters

The Yorkie's small size makes traveling convenient, feeding inexpensive, and exercising easy. But it also makes the Yorkie a less than

stellar protection dog, marathon jogging companion, or rough and tumble playmate. Tiny dogs are easily tripped over and easily injured. They

Yorkies can be close companions for responsible youngsters.

Small Talk
World's Smallest?

A Yorkie named Whitney, at 750 grams and 6 inches in length, holds the individual record as world's smallest dog. Her owner says she drinks out of an egg cup and is petrified of cats. The previous record holder was Big Boss, also a Yorkie, who stood 4.7 inches tall. Pinnochio, a 1-pound Yorkie, is currently challenging the record.

Tiny Yorkies are cute, but they require special care.

are more susceptible to cold weather, missed meals, and certain health problems.

Many people are drawn to the tiniest Yorkies, and some less ethical breeders try to cash in by advertising "teacup" Yorkies. No separate teacup type of Yorkie exists, and despite the undeniable appeal of a teeny dog, especially small Yorkies have several drawbacks. Yorkies are already pushing the envelope as far as size and health are concerned; choosing the tiniest of an already tiny breed magnifies the chance and severity of health problems such as hypoglycemia (page 32), moleras (page 16), hydrocephalus (page 97), and tooth loss (page 82), and injuries. Because tiny puppies may not thrive as well as larger ones, they are not suited for inexperienced small dog owners.

The Yorkie standard gives no preference for smaller dogs within the 7-pound weight limit. If you want to compete in obedience, agility, or other performance sports with your Yorkie, a dog near the top of the allowed weight limit will generally have an easier time. Even conformation dogs may be hindered by tiny size, as many shows are held outdoors where even moderately tall grass can hinder movement. Larger Yorkies are better suited as children's playmates. A Yorkie near the upper weight limit is a better choice for breeding (but first consider the caveats on page 124); it's too dangerous to breed a Yorkie female weighing less than 3 or 4 pounds. You can get a rough idea of a puppy's eventual adult height and weight by doubling the puppy's height and weight at 13 weeks of age.

Meet Your Match

It's not hard to find a Yorkshire Terrier, but if you want one that represents the breed at its finest, you can hedge your bet by choosing your source carefully. To do that, you need to know how to tell good breeders from bad breeders, and good Yorkies from even better Yorkies.

Everyone wants a good, healthy companion; in addition, some people want a competitive show or agility dog. Most healthy Yorkies can make good obedience or agility prospects, but Yorkies suffering from orthopedic problems such as patellar luxation (see page 94) are at a disadvantage. The same is true for conformation prospects—and for

Small Talk
Puppy Coats

One of the Yorkie's most distinctive qualities is its fine, glossy, long coat of unusual metallic shades. If you want your Yorkie to look like a show dog, you need to choose one from parents with such coats. The Yorkshire Terrier breed standard calls for adult body coat color of dark steel punctuated with clear tan points. The blue should not be black or silver or mingled with other colors. The tan also should not be mingled with other colors. But the puppies you're looking at will be dogs of a different color!

Yorkie pups are born black with tan points (meaning tan on the muzzle, above each eye, at the base and rims of the ears, under the tail, on the chest, and on each foot extending part way up each leg. Small white marks that may be present on the chest, head, or feet will disappear with maturity, but larger patches probably will remain. Pups that are born all black, all tan, all gray, gray and tan, spotted, or anything but black and tan will never develop the proper coloration.

Only when the adult coat comes in will they begin to sport their adult colors. Experienced breeders may be able to predict which pups will have proper coloring by examining the shade of gold on its ears or head, but even so, it is an inexact science.

The adult Yorkie should have a long straight coat, but such coats take a long time to grow. It's tempting to choose the pup with the thickest, heaviest coat, but such pups tend to grow into adults with dull coats of incorrect wooly or cottony texture. The pup with the thin, silky coat will have the correct texture as an adult.

pets. Good health is vitally important and partly hereditary.

Nobody can guarantee a dog will live a long and healthy life, but you can increase your odds by choosing a dog from a healthy family. Ask about the longevity of your potential puppy's ancestors. Ask in particular about patellar luxation, portosystemic (or liver) shunts, tracheal collapse, patent ductus arteriosis, Legg-Calve'-Perthes disease, and urinary stones. These are all conditions to which Yorkies seem predisposed, and which may have a hereditary basis. The best breeders have their dogs checked clear of these conditions before breeding them. They may provide veterinary certification or, for patellar luxation, an Orthopedic Foundation for Animals (OFA) number. No line of dogs is perfect, so don't discount a line with some problems. Besides, some other breeders may not be as honest in disclosing problems.

The Yorkie is known for its glossy coat in shades of dark steel and clear tan.

If you want a male for conformation or breeding, be sure he has both testicles descended into the scrotum by the time you take him home. They should both be down by 8 weeks of age, although some may be as late as 16 weeks (or in rare cases, longer—but don't bank on it).

Just as important as good health is a good temperament. You want a Yorkie because you want a loving, confident companion. Excessively shy Yorkies may not be able to enjoy as many activities with you. Some Yorkies may come from genetically shy stock or from socially isolated environments, both of which can make them more challenging to shape into confident adults. You can increase your chance of getting a Yorkie with a good temperament by getting a home-raised Yorkie from parents with good temperaments. Obedience or agility titles (see pages 113 and 116) are one sign of good temperaments, but nothing beats meeting the parents yourself.

Don't forget looks! Part of the appeal of the Yorkshire Terrier is its petite size, glorious coat, intriguing color, and entrancing expression. Breeders concerned with producing conformation competition Yorkies are most likely to produce Yorkies with the appearance that drew you to the breed. Examine the pedigree for close relatives with conformation championships. Get to know the Yorkie standard and look at top winning Yorkies. You won't need a top show dog pedigree unless you plan to compete in conformation. Nonetheless, conformation breeders often have Yorkies available that are not quite show quality, but nonetheless often so close only an expert could tell. Such dogs have the benefit of being raised with the best of knowledge and care.

Looking for a Little Love

Most people seeking a Yorkie don't want a competition dog, just a new best friend. They look to newspaper ads, friends, pet stores, breed connoisseurs, and rescue. Unfortunately, some of the sources are not good choices. Newspaper ads are usually placed by naïve breeders who know nothing about genetics, health, or puppy care. Some ads are placed by high-volume breeders

Small Talk
Rare Deals

Don't be fooled by tales of "rare" silver or spotted or other nonstandard Yorkie colors, or of doll-faced or teacup-sized Yorkies. Yorkies occasionally come in colors besides the accepted ones, but they're uncommon because breeders have selected against these colors for generations. *Baby doll* or *doll-faced* refers to a head with a shorter muzzle, rounder shape, and rounder eye than the Yorkshire Terrier standard calls for. Although cute, they are not technically correct from a purist point of view. Teacup Yorkies refer to exceptionally small Yorkies, but they are not a special type of Yorkie. Because they can be challenging to raise (see page 124) most serious breeders do not intentionally try to produce such small dogs. If these traditionally nonpreferred traits are

traits you prefer, then don't hesitate to seek them out, but don't expect to impress breed purists with them. Most responsible breeders avoid producing such Yorkies, and when they do, they don't promote them as rare or exotic.

A good Yorkie is one that fits the Yorkie standard and has a good temperament and good health. If you prefer something not in the standard, that's your choice; just don't pay extra in the belief that it's superior. By the same token, don't be impressed by puppies imported from far away, even overseas. Yorkie pups are tiny and can be shipped great distances at little expense; unscrupulous wholesalers will buy entire litters cheaply from abroad in hopes of selling them at a great profit.

who use dogs to make money with little regard for their welfare or quality. They may field calls for a number of breeds and then hustle one of their many litters to a home where they pose as family-raised puppies. Breed connoisseurs, often called hobby breeders, are the best choice if you want the best Yorkie. Rescue organizations are the best choice if you want to make a difference.

Hobby breeders dedicate their efforts to producing high-quality dogs. To do this, they prove their

dogs in some form of competition and screen them for hereditary health problems. Nonetheless, not every puppy is competition quality. These pet-quality puppies still profit from the breeder's knowledge of genetics and puppy care and are available to qualified homes. Good hobby breeders will expect you to keep them abreast of your puppy's progress and come to them for the duration of your Yorkie's life.

Hobby breeders can be located through Yorkshire Terrier clubs, dog

Yorkie puppies don't look like adults!

magazines (especially Yorkshire Terrier magazines), or kennel pages on the internet. A good place to find good breeders is at a dog show or even better, a Yorkshire Terrier specialty show (a prestigious show in which only Yorkies compete). The annual Yorkshire Terrier Club of America National specialty is held each February in New York City right before the Westminster show. Another National specialty is held in a different location each year. Large specialties attract hundreds of top competitors in conformation and performance events.

Some breeders are more ethical and knowledgeable than others, and some advertisements are more truthful than others. Visit prospective breeders personally and see for yourself how their dogs look and act and how their puppies are being raised. Look for these signs of a responsible breeder:

- Raises puppies in the home, not in a kennel building or garage.
- Has puppies and adults that seem acclimated to living as part of the family, rather than in cages or pens.
- Has outgoing, confident adults and puppies with temperaments you like.
- Has clean, well-groomed, healthy-appearing dogs.
- Is familiar with and screens for Yorkshire Terrier health concerns.
- Can compare her dogs to the breed standard feature by feature.
- Charges neither bargain basement nor exorbitant prices.
- Has the mother of the litter available to meet.
- Has photos and pedigrees of both parents and other relatives.
- Has registration papers available at the time of purchase.
- Breeds sparingly and dedicates her breeding efforts to only one or two breeds.
- Belongs to a Yorkshire Terrier club.
- Is involved in some sort of Yorkie competitive or service activity.
- Asks you lots of questions about your past history with dogs, facilities, family, life style, and expectations for your new dog.
- Can tell you about how puppies from former litters are doing and provide references from former puppy-buyers.
- Won't allow puppies to leave until they are at least 10 or preferably 12 weeks old.

• Does not require puppy-back agreements that require you to breed the dog.

• Doesn't pressure you into buying a puppy, especially if you asked to think about it first.

• Requires that, should you ever have to relinquish the dog, she gets first refusal.

• Provides a medical history, pedigree, registration information, and written care instructions with each puppy.

• Agrees that the sale is contingent on your veterinarian checking the puppy within the first 2 days you have it.

Rescues: You may have planned and studied to find the perfect Yorkie. But sometimes the best dogs find us. They present themselves when we are looking for quite a different dog. They insert themselves into our lives when we least expect it. They burrow into our hearts when we thought we had no more room. Somehow they stay when we vowed they were just visiting—and we never know how we got along without them. They are the rescues, and they make us realize how special and perfect every Yorkie is.

The popularity of the Yorkshire Terrier, combined with the tendency of people to impulse buy and to underestimate the work involved in caring for a dog, has created an overabundance of Yorkies needing new families. They come in all descriptions and have varied histories, but the typical rescue Yorkie is a nice dog who simply had the misfortune to be consid-ered expendable by her former family. Some come from traumatic backgrounds, and some come from loving homes that simply could not keep them, too often because they could not housetrain them. The advantage of working with a rescue organization is that they will know the dog's background and any potential problems. To offer a Yorkie in need of a place in your home and heart, contact your local Yorkie club or a Yorkshire Terrier Rescue group listed on page 148.

Age of consent: Responsible Yorkie breeders often won't place puppies until they are at least 10 or even 12 weeks old, especially to inexperienced homes. This is because Yorkie puppies are so tiny that they are more vulnerable to the stress of changing homes. Very small puppies should stay with the breeder even longer.

The parents are the best guide to how their offspring will mature.

Whether rescue or show dog, personality defines the Yorkshire Terrier!

Small Talk
Moleras

Some Yorkies, especially tiny ones, will have a soft spot on top of the skull where the parts of the skull have not yet knitted together. This spot, called a molera or open fontanel, will usually disappear by about 6 months of age, but in some cases it will remain for life. Extra vigilance must be taken with such dogs to avoid hitting them in the head or having them hit themselves on furniture corners. Most Yorkies with moleras live hardy lives.

A puppy is not always the best choice. Breeders may have available adult dogs that would relish the chance to live as pampered pets. Adults are often already house-trained—but don't count on it! In fact, it may be more difficult to housetrain an adult who has been raised as a kennel dog.

Papers and pedigrees: If having a registered dog is important to you, understanding the registry is just as important. Most Yorkies in North America are registered with the American Kennel Club, United Kennel Club (UKC), or Canadian Kennel Club (CKC). Many other registries, even with the same initials, have no requirements, and registration with them is meaningless.

Even registration with a respected organization is not an endorsement of quality. It simply certifies that the dog is of pure Yorkshire Terrier breeding. Often a breeder will sell a pet-quality dog with a Limited Registration, which means that if the dog is bred, the AKC will not register its offspring. Breeders do this for dogs that they believe are not breeding quality in case the new owners don't have the dog neutered or spayed. AKC also offers Indefinite Listing Privilege (ILP) registration to spayed or neutered dogs that are obviously Yorkshire Terriers but lack the paperwork to prove it. Dogs with Limited Registration or ILP numbers can compete in all AKC competitions except conformation.

How much for that doggy? Well-bred and raised Yorkshire Terriers are

Good luck choosing!

not cheap. Although a dog from a responsible breeder may seem expensive compared to one from a backyard breeder, consider what has gone into the production of this puppy. The parents' health clearances, championships, and other titles cost the breeder a lot of money, time, and effort to obtain. The parents themselves were not cheap dogs because their parents in turn had health clearances and titles. The breeder probably paid a stud fee and possibly shipping fees to breed to the best male available rather than the closest one. Pre-breeding health tests, ovulation testing, and prenatal care (which may include fetal monitoring, radiographs, and ultrasound) can be costly, as can a caesarean section. Responsible

breeders make many sacrifices to produce quality Yorkies; their commitment doesn't end when you walk out the door. You're not just buying a better puppy; you're buying a puppy with the best start possible in life, and you're buying the breeder's advice for the duration of that puppy's life.

Cheaper puppies are available from backyard breeders who have never heard of Yorkie health problems; wouldn't know if their dogs had them; have minimal money, time, or effort invested in the litter; and have even less advice to offer after you've left with your puppy. This doesn't mean that you can't get a wonderful companion from a naïve breeder, but you do get something extra from a responsible breeder.

Don't confuse price with quality. Unscrupulous "puppy mills" churn out as many puppies as possible while investing as little as they can in them, in turn wholesaling them to retailers who charge top dollar. No matter what your source, compare the puppies you see to the points that follow.

Puppy Picking

Because Yorkie litters are small—typically only three puppies—you may have to wait to get a puppy from a good breeder, and even then there will be few puppies to choose among. Young Yorkshire Terriers should be curious, alert, and self-confident. A puppy that freezes or always heads home when carried away from her littermates may not have the self-confidence of the typical Yorkie. For most family companions, your best option is choose neither the boldest nor the shyest puppy. Many people who can't decide let the puppy pick them. It's hard to say no to a tousled tyke that tumbles over to say hello and ends up falling asleep in your lap. Of course, you may be in big trouble if you end up with a whole lap full!

Your prospective puppy should
• Have her first vaccinations and deworming.
• Be outgoing and active. Avoid an overly fearful or aggressive puppy. If a puppy is apathetic or sleepy, it could be that she just ate, but it could also be a sign of sickness.

• Be clean, with no missing hair, crusted or reddened skin, or signs of parasites.
• Have no indication of redness or irritation around the anus, which indicates diarrhea.
• Have pink gums; pale gums may indicate anemia.
• Not be coughing, sneezing, or vomiting.
• Not be thin or pot-bellied, which could indicate internal parasites.
• Have clean eyes, ears, and nostrils, free of any discharge.
• Not be dehydrated, which can suggest repeated vomiting or diarrhea. Test for dehydration by picking up a fold of skin and releasing it. The skin should "pop" back into place.
• Not have rear dewclaws. Some Yorkies are born with extra toes on the inside of the hind legs; because these can be injured by getting caught on things, reputable breeders remove them at birth.

You've studied the breed and know you are willing to take on the responsibility of a very special breed of dog. You've searched for a reputable breeder, by-passing the newspaper ads and other easily accessible sources in favor of breeders who have dedicated their lives to producing healthy dogs representative of the best this breed has to offer. You've found the litter that comes closest to meeting your ideals, and finally selected the puppy of your dreams. Now make those dreams come true . . .

Chapter Three

Your Yorkie Youngster

You are embarking on the adventure of a lifetime with your Yorkie companion. You will learn from each other, test each other, and appreciate each other in new ways every day. Your Yorkie will share your life and your home, and to do so, he'll have to follow certain rules of etiquette.

Welcome Home

Some people say preparing for a puppy is like preparing for a baby, but those people are wrong. No baby can gut the sofa, squeeze into ductwork, gnaw through a chair leg, eat his own body weight in garbage, or dance nimbly from your reach. A 2-pound Yorkie baby can do more damage and be more damaged than any human baby.

Yorkie puppies are explorers. They will investigate parts of your house you haven't cleaned in years, become intimately acquainted with the undersides of your furniture, and be lured by the treasures of your trash. You need to see the house from the Yorkie point of view to prevent carnage before it happens.

Yorkie puppies prune your houseplants to the roots, decorate your shoes with intricate teeth mark patterns, and moisturize and fertilize as much carpeting as their digestive systems will allow. They can damage both your home and themselves. Yorkies often explore with their teeth, and any chewed items in his wake are your fault, not his—you are the one who should know better. Puppies can gnaw through electrical cords, lick electrical outlets, and tug on electrical cords until they pull over a lamp. They can be crushed in slamming doors, be caught in swinging doors, run full speed into invisible glass doors, break through screen doors, or escape from open doors.

Yorkies are gifted jumpers. They love to survey their kingdom from a high perch, and they insist on leaping to your lap or onto your bed. What they jump onto, they jump off of. Not only can they hurt themselves jumping from furniture, but they can also fall from decks or down stairs. Fence off any high areas and consider making ramps leading to beds or chairs. These can be elaborate ramps with rails, or simply a stack of pillows.

The essence of cute...

Otherwise teach your Yorkie to stay until you lift her down.

Dangers abound outdoors. Check for poisonous plants, bushes with sharp, broken branches at Yorkie eye level, and trees with dead branches or heavy fruits or pine cones in danger of falling. If you have a pool, be aware that, although Yorkies can swim, they can't do so for long and can't get out a pool without help. Even if the pool has steps, they won't know where to find them unless they've had lots of practice. Tiny dogs are at the mercy of predatory wildlife. Don't leave your Yorkie in an outside area where coyotes, mountain lions, or large birds can be tempted. If you live in a wildlife area consider using a covered run or yard.

Accessorize

Your new Yorkie may be dwarfed by all the items in your Yorkie welcome basket—but that's half the fun of bringing home a new dog! You'll need a leash and collar, grooming equipment, food, bowls, and lots of toys!

Collars: Yorkies look dazzling bejeweled in the finest collars. But for everyday wear, many people find cat collars work well with Yorkies. Buckle collars can slip over the dog's head, which could be disastrous when walking near a road. A well-fitting slip ("choke") or martingale collar won't slip over the head but can choke your dog if it's snagged on

20

something while you're not watching. These collars are only for use when you're attached to the other end!

Some Yorkies prefer a dapper-looking harness. A harness has several advantages. It can't slip off, be backed out of, choke a dog, or irritate the throat. The latter is especially important in dogs predisposed to tracheal collapse (see page 89). In an emergency, you can safely lift a dog in the air by his harness. Some show breeders warn that constant use of a harness may cause the elbows to spread away from the body, which would be detrimental to a show dog's career, but this shouldn't matter to most Yorkies.

A well-fitting collar or harness with tags can help reunite you with your lost Yorkie. More permanent means of identification include a tattoo with your social security number or her AKC number on the inner thigh, or a microchip implant. A microchip contains information that can be read by a scanner that animal shelters use. Information for both tattoos and microchips is stored in a central registry.

A Safe Haven

Yorkies are people dogs. They need to be not just in the house but also in the thick of things. They won't be happy banished to the garage or laundry room. Actually, they won't be happy until they've taken over your home and claimed it as their own. Your job is to come up with a com-

Small Print
In the Swim

If you have a pool, fence it securely so that your Yorkie can't fall in. Even so, take the time to teach your Yorkie to swim to the steps or some platform for safety. Many Yorkies enjoy a brief swim. To encourage swimming, entice your dog to go with you into a child's wading pool filled with just a few inches of water at first. Gradually increase the water depth. After the water is over her head, help her swim by elevating her rear so that she won't be splashing on top of the water with her front paws. Never let a Yorkie swim alone, and be careful that a long-coated dog doesn't get the coat tangled on something under water. Swimming is an excellent exercise for dogs with arthritis or limb injuries. Of course, most Yorkies prefer just soaking up the rays poolside or sharing your float.

promise. Your Yorkie needs limits at first, for his own safety as well as your home's. Use baby gates to shut off areas that are not for Yorkie occupancy. Use exercise pens to limit your Yorkie to a small area inside when you can't watch him carefully. And use a cage (crate) when he needs to be confined to bed.

A private den: Your Yorkie needs a place he can call his own, a place he can seek out whenever he needs rest and solitude, a place he will be safe when left alone or during hectic

Small Talk
Yorkie Stuff

- Food and water bowls: stainless steel bowls are best, followed by ceramic. Plastic can cause allergic reactions in some dogs.
- Food: start with what the breeder has been feeding your dog and gradually change to the brand you prefer.
- Collar: a cat collar may be best.
- Harness: a safe choice for walks.
- Lightweight leash: a cat leash or an adjustable show lead works well.
- Lightweight retractable leash: more freedom without danger.
- Toys: latex squeakies, fleece toys, ball, stuffed animals, stuffed socks (especially stuffed with crackly sounding paper), or empty plastic soda jugs. Make sure that no squeakers or plastic parts can be pulled off and swallowed.
- Chewbones: the equivalent of a baby's teething ring.
- Anti-chew sprays. The unpleasant taste dissuades puppies from chewing.

- Cage ("crate"): it should be large enough for an adult Yorkie to stand up in.
- Exercise pen: a handy indoor yard.
- Baby gates: avoid accordion-style gates, which can close around a dog's neck.
- Nail clippers: guillotine-type clippers are easier to use.
- Brush and comb (see page 62).
- Dog shampoo (see page 68).
- First aid kit (see page 102).
- Poop scoop: a two-piece rake type is best for grass.
- Dog coat or sweater: Yorkies have no undercoat, so their long hair provides little insulation from the cold. Their small size also increases heat loss because they have greater surface area compared to volume than large dogs do. In short, Yorkies get cold! Besides, they wear clothes well.

household happenings. He needs a crate. Don't expect him to stay crated all day. The crate is not a babysitter, punishment, or storage box.

Used correctly, the crate can be an important asset. Place it in a quiet place not too far from family activities. Place a snuggly bed or blanket inside. Place him inside when he begins to fall asleep. When he awakens, take him immediately to his potty area.

Travel cage: Your Yorkie should never be allowed the run of your car. He can get tangled in the steering wheel, get caught under the brake, be thrown into the dash, be hit by an airbag, or fall out the window. Attach a small cage to your seat so that it remains secure, and place him in it whenever he rides.

X-pen: X-pens (exercise pens) are transportable folding wire playpens for dogs, typically about 4 feet by

4 feet. They allow room for the puppy to relieve himself on paper or in a litterbox in one corner, to sleep on a soft bed in the other, and to frolic with his toys all over! The X-pen provides a safe time-out area when you just need some quiet time for yourself or a safe holding area when you must be gone for a long time.

Fence: Many Yorkies are apartment dogs, but if you have the facilities, a fenced outside area leading from the back door is a big help in raising and housetraining a dog. Make sure that your fence is absolutely Yorkie-proof from the outset. Yorkies are accomplished diggers and squeezers, and after they dig under or squeeze through a fence once, they learn to look even harder for vulnerable spots. For your dog's safety and your own peace of mind, get a fence you never have to worry about. A tiny dog loose in a big world won't get many second chances.

Invisible fences are not advisable for Yorkies. The collar they must wear is too heavy, the shock they receive from crossing the boundary is too intense, and the protection a real fence affords them against marauding dogs and dognappers is absent.

Raising Havoc

Now is one of the most important times in your Yorkie's life. It's your responsibility to guide this blue tornado to becoming a well-mannered and well-socialized canine companion.

Don't bring a new puppy home during the hectic holidays.

Housetraining: Yorkies, like many toy dogs, can be a challenge to housetrain. Proper housetraining can mean more than the difference between a pristine carpet and a soggy one; it could mean the difference between a life shared with a special friend and one spent in frustration. Lack of housetraining is the single greatest behavior problem causing people to give up their Yorkies.

Several theories have been offered for why toy dogs have problems with housebreaking. One is that most toys are raised exclusively indoors. Their breeders may raise them in a whelping box or X-pen, finding it easier to clean up their

Keep plants out of reach for their safety and your Yorkie's!

You can't teach your puppy the proper place to do his business if he's running amuck and letting loose every time he feels inclined. Restricting his freedom by using a crate trains him to hold himself for short periods because dogs have a natural desire to avoid soiling their denning area. By taking him directly outside from the crate upon awakening, it teaches him the proper place to use for his bathroom duties.

Dogs have limits to how long they can hold themselves. A rule of thumb is that a puppy can, at most, hold his bowels for as many hours as the puppy is months old. This means that a three-month old puppy can hold himself for three hours. But a toy dog may not be able to go that long. If the puppy is forced to stay in a crate longer than he can hold himself, you are training him to soil his crate and negating its usefulness.

Don't just shove the puppy out the door. He will spend his time outside standing at the door. Go with him, and when he relieves himself, heap on the praise and give him a treat. Then you can bring him back inside to play. But remember, he'll need to go out even more after he's played.

If you live in an apartment, consider litter-box training your Yorkie. Special absorbent dog litter that entices dogs to use it is available. Take the puppy to the box just as you would take him outdoors. If he starts to go outside the box, quickly hustle him into it. Then praise lavishly for this mighty accomplishment!

small mess a few times a day than to hustle them in and out the door and guard them against outdoor dangers. Next, most new Yorkie owners give their dogs too much freedom in the house. It's easy to miss a little dog squatting, and just as easy to overlook the tiny puddles, and new owners may not realize the extent of the problem until the behavior has become ingrained. Finally, it may be that toy dogs simply don't achieve bladder control at as early an age as do larger dogs. Their owners, upon hearing how their neighbor's dog is housetrained at 8 weeks of age while their Yorkie is still oblivious to the concept at 8 months, grow frustrated and may give up and banish the dog to a pen or a room with a tile floor.

Yorkies can swim, but must always be closely supervised while they are in the water.

ing and soon after heavy drinking or playing he needs to urinate. Right after eating, or if nervous, he will probably need to defecate. Circling, whining, sniffing, and generally acting worried usually signals that defecation is imminent.

When he does have an accident, just say "No," quickly scoop him up, and place him in his potty area. Overly stern corrections teach him not to relieve himself in your presence, even outside. Punishing him for a mess he made earlier only convinces him that every once in a while, for no apparent reason, you are apt to go insane and attack him. That "guilty" look you may think your dog is exhibiting is really fear that you will once again lose your mind.

Because dogs are creatures of habit, housetraining is more a matter of prevention than correction. To avoid accidents, learn to predict when your puppy needs to relieve himself. Immediately after awaken-

The Yorkie socialite: Yorkies are social animals so they need to learn social graces. Even if you live alone, your Yorkie needs to learn to interact

Standard dog toys tend to be too large for Yorkie puppies.

with other people and other dogs. She should meet new people and see new sights during her formative puppy months. That doesn't mean she has to go to parties and crowds; in fact, just the opposite is true. She should meet a variety of people in nonstressful, calm situations.

Puppy kindergarten classes give youngsters a chance to learn how to interact with people and other dogs. Good classes allow puppies to interact in a structured environment, preventing bullying and fighting while encouraging tolerance and confidence. Yorkie puppies are confronted by a strange new world filled with human and canine rules. Puppy kindergarten helps them learn both.

Children: Yorkies are child magnets, so you must ensure that your Yorkie isn't overwhelmed by a crowd of children all trying to pet her at once. Children should be seated

Your Yorkie will need a bed of his own.

on the floor when playing with a Yorkie so that they can't drop or step on the dog. They must be taught that Yorkies can't be dropped, hit in the head, encouraged to jump off furniture, stepped on, fallen upon, or yanked off the ground in an overly vigorous game of tug-of-war. Responsible, experienced children will learn to be careful enough to play traditional dog games outside, but for now, your puppy must be sheltered from accidents and overzealous handling.

Introduce adult Yorkies and children carefully, encouraging the child to offer the dog a treat. If you take things slowly and calmly, most Yorkies will come to enjoy children.

Any dog must be carefully supervised around babies. Introduce the dog to the baby gradually, rewarding her for being calm and well mannered. Always praise the dog when the baby is present. Never shuttle her out of the room because the baby is coming in. You want the dog to associate the baby with good times; you don't want her to be resentful. Remember, your Yorkie thought she was the baby of the family!

Dogs: Most Yorkies get along with other dogs, although the Yorkie's terrier heritage ensures that cohabitation will never be dull. Problems between canine housemates are more likely to occur between dogs of the same sex and age. Seniority counts for a lot in the dog world, and a young puppy will usually grow up respecting his elders.

True to his terrier heritage, the Yorkie can be very territorial.

While rough play and occasional flared tempers are natural, repeated disagreements that leave one dog screaming or bleeding, or in which the dogs cannot be readily separated, spell trouble. Neutering one or both males in a dominance dispute can sometimes help, but neutering females seldom helps.

It's human nature to soothe the underdog and punish the bully, but that does the underdog no favor. If they are fighting for dominance, they are doing so partly for your favor. If you give it to the underdog, the aggressor will only try harder to earn your favor by getting rid of the wrongful heir. Instead, treat the top dog like a king and the losing dog like a prince. This means you greet, pet, and feed the top dog first. That doesn't mean you reward either for fighting; if a fight breaks out, separate them as quickly as possible either by pulling them apart or by throwing water on them. Express your displeasure and separate them for a short time. Reintroduce them soon after and make sure that they are both distracted with a treat or a chance to go for a walk.

Going for a long walk together in neutral territory, with each dog leashed, is an ideal way for dogs to get acquainted and form a pleasurable association. Prevent an aggressive dog from excessive marking with urine during the walk. Dogs

Supervise interactions between puppies and children.

mark their territory by urinating on various posts; the more he marks, the more he will tend to behave aggressively toward other dogs in that area.

The Yorkie penchant for thinking big can get him into big trouble with big dogs. Yorkies think nothing of

"You want me to do what where?"

approaching and even challenging strange dogs with all the cockiness of a street fighter. This tough façade is often enough to intimidate big dogs, but not always. No matter how tough your Yorkie, he's not going to win a real fight against a full-size dog.

Some large dogs start fights, and some view Yorkies as prey animals. Many breeds of dogs were bred to run down small, fast-moving mammals, and they may not realize a Yorkie is a dog until it's too late. Safeguard your Yorkie around large dogs by keeping him on a lead and carrying a little protective dog carrier, a big stick, or pepper spray. One reason that it's a good idea to use a harness when walking your Yorkie is that it's easier to pull him away from danger and even into your arms by his chest, rather than his neck.

Animals: Yorkies may be a bit less predictable around other animals. Many Yorkies are true to their terrier heritage by seeking out quarry to catch and adversaries to confront. Your Yorkie won't hesitate to chase a wild animal. If you have pet rodents, you must protect them from your Yorkie.

Introduce other family pets carefully. If you have a cat, feed them together, and don't allow either one to run after or from the other. Make sure that more entertaining things are available to distract your Yorkie. After they get used to one another, Yorkies and cats can become close friends.

"You want a sample of my what?"

Yorkie Pediatrics

Like all youngsters, Yorkie puppies need your help to grow up healthy. Your veterinarian can guide you through the best preventive health care regime for your dog, including vaccinations, deworming, and possibly neutering or spaying.

Vaccinations: Your puppy will need to be vaccinated before he ventures out into a world full of viruses and disease. Puppies receive their dam's immunity from colostrum, the special type of milk she produces in the first days of life. This passive immunity wears off after several weeks, but there's no way to know exactly when. If it wears off, your puppy will be vulnerable; but if vaccinations are given before it wears off, they won't be effective,

and your puppy will be equally vulnerable. Thus, a series of vaccinations are given in order to catch the immune system at the earliest time the vaccinations will take effect.

Nothing is gained by vaccinating too much, or by vaccinating an already ill dog. Vaccinations occasionally cause adverse reactions, especially in toy dogs. Some toy dog breeders report fewer adverse effects by using smaller vaccine dosages. However, veterinary consensus is that tiny dogs require the same vaccine dose as giant dogs. This is because stimulation of the body's immune system doesn't depend on the concentration of the vaccine in the body, but rather the absolute amount of vaccine.

Vaccinations are divided into core vaccines, which are advisable for all dogs, and noncore vaccines, which

Rest is as important as exercise for young ones.

are advisable for only some dogs. Core vaccines are those for rabies, distemper, parvovirus, and hepatitis (using the CAV-2 vaccine). Noncore vaccines include those for leptospirosis, corona virus, tracheobronchitis, Lyme disease, and giardia. Your veterinarian can advise you if your dog is at risk for these diseases.

Veterinary organizations have recently revised their vaccination protocols to include fewer booster shots. One such protocol suggests giving a three-shot series for puppies, each shot containing distemper (or measles for the first series), parvovirus, adenovirus 2 (CAV-2), parainfluenza (CPIV), and distemper, with one rabies vaccination at 16 weeks. Following this a booster is given one year later, and then subsequent boosters are given every 3 years.

Deworming: Internal parasites can be devastating for a tiny puppy. The number one prevention for most worms is daily removal of feces from the yard. Some heartworm preventives also prevent most types of intestinal worms (but not tapeworms). Over-the-counter dewormers are neither as effective nor as safe as those available from your veterinarian. A stool check can determine the type of parasite your dog may have and direct the veterinarian to the best treatment for it. For these reasons, your Yorkie should be dewormed only under the supervision of your veterinarian.

Even puppies from the most fastidious breeders can get worms because some types of larval worms can lie dormant and safe from deworming in the dam long before she ever became pregnant, awaiting hormonal changes caused by her pregnancy to become active and infect her puppies. Your dog may also pick up worms from areas where lots of dogs congregate.

The most common intestinal parasites are ascarids, hookworms, whipworms, and protozoa such as coccidia and giardia. Diarrhea, weight loss, and other signs can signal the presence of any of these parasites. The best way to detect them is with a fecal check.

Heartworm prevention: Heartworms are killers. Wherever mosquitoes are present, dogs should be on heartworm prevention. Your puppy should start taking the preventive at an early age; the exact time will depend on her exposure to mosquitoes. Monthly preventives don't stay in the dog's system for a month, but instead act on a particular stage in the heartworm's development. Giving the drug each month prevents any heartworms from ever maturing. The most common way of checking for heartworms is to check the blood for circulating microfilarae (the immature form of heartworms), but this method may fail to detect the presence of adult heartworms in as many as 20 percent of all tested dogs. More accurate is an occult heartworm test, which detects antigens to heartworms in the blood. With either test, the presence of heartworms will not be detectable until nearly 7 months after infection. Heartworms are treatable in their early stages, but the treatment is expensive and not without risk.

Spaying and neutering: You will probably find life easier if your Yorkie is spayed or neutered. If you think you'd like to breed a litter, first consider all the reasons not to breed (page 124). An intact (unspayed) female will come into estrus, or season, usually around 8 months of age. This will last for about 3 weeks, during which she will have a bloody discharge that can stain your furnishings. Part of that time she will be enticing and receptive to males, so you must keep them separated. Intact (unneutered) males seldom suffer in silence and can make your life miserable. A month or two after her season she will often have a false pregnancy, which can be so convincing you will wonder where you slipped up. She may have milk and even adopt a toy as though it were a baby.

Besides your mental health, canine health reasons exist for spaying and neutering. Intact females are at increased risk of developing pyometra, a potentially fatal infection of the uterus, and breast cancer. Spaying before her first season drastically reduces the chance of breast cancer

Most Yorkies are better off being pets, not parents.

Now is the time to familiarize your puppy with grooming.

in later life. Intact male dogs are more likely to roam or fight. They are also more likely to develop testicular cancer. The major drawbacks are that some neutered or spayed dogs gain weight and that some spayed females can develop urinary incontinence. Talk to your veterinarian about the pros and cons and the best time to have the procedure performed.

Baby Food

Feeding any puppy is important; feeding a Yorkie puppy is critical. Your Yorkie should eat a high-quality puppy food many times a day. Poor feeding practices can lead not only to poor nutrition, poor growth, and poor health but also to a potentially fatal condition called hypoglycemia.

Hypoglycemia: Hypoglycemia is a disorder of the central nervous system caused by low blood sugar. It occurs most often in small, young, stressed, or active dogs, such as Yorkie puppies. These dogs aren't able to store enough readily available glucose, so when the available glycogen (the form in which the body stores glucose) is depleted, the body begins to break down energy stored in fat. Small puppies have little subcutaneous fat, however, so that energy is soon depleted. When that happens, the brain, which depends on glucose-derived energy to function, ceases to function properly. Signs such as sleepiness, weakness, and loss of appetite and coordination may appear suddenly. Left untreated, the condition can worsen until the dog has seizures, loses consciousness, and dies.

A Yorkie puppy under the age of 7 months should not go more than 4 hours without eating. Because this is seldom practical in the middle of the night, they should be kept warm and confined at night so that they don't expend a lot of energy playing and barking.

Meals should be fairly high in protein, fat, and complex carbohydrates. Complex carbohydrates slow the breakdown of carbohydrates into sugars, which should lead to more efficient utilization. Avoid semi-moist foods because of their high sugar content, as well as other simple sugars such as syrup unless your dog is already showing signs of hypoglycemia.

If you suspect that your dog is having a hypoglycemic episode, immediately feed him a food high in sugar content such as corn syrup or even honey (Karo syrup is recommended). If the dog can't eat, rub syrup on his gums and the roof of his mouth, but don't try to put anything down his throat because he could choke. Keep him warm. You should see improvement within 2 minutes; use this time to alert your veterinarian that you are bringing him in immediately for treatment, possibly with intravenous glucose. After he is stronger and can swallow, it's important to immediately give him a small, high-protein meal, such as beef or chicken baby food.

Hypoglycemia is mostly a problem of puppies (it may be related to immaturity of liver cells), and most Yorkies will outgrow it by the time they reach about 7 months of age. All Yorkie owners should be aware of the symptoms and treatments for the entire life of their dog, however, especially in times of stress. Feed your Yorkie, especially your young Yorkie, regular, frequent meals.

Puppy Grooming

Because grooming will be an important part of your Yorkie's life, now is the time to accustom him to how pleasant the experience can be. Gently stroke him with a soft brush. He may try to bite the brush in play; if so, brush him for a few more strokes and then wait until he's sleepier and try again. You can start with him in your lap, but eventually

A Yorkie has even been a war hero!

Small Talk
Ears

The ears of most Yorkies will stand upright by 6 to 8 weeks of age, but some take a little longer, and some need a little help. Larger ears will usually have more difficulty standing, but don't give up—at least not until he's 6 months old. You can help train ears to stand by giving them some support. Begin by carefully shaving away the hair on the top third or half of the ears, both front and back. Be very careful; you can shave in the same pattern described for adults (page 65). Next use masking tape to tape the ears so that they are folded in on themselves vertically and come to a point at the top. It will take a few tries before you get it tight enough to withstand his pawing at it, but not so tight that it cuts off his circulation. Err on the side of too loose and plan on doing it again—and again. You may also tape the two taped ears together so that they stand upright. Remove the tape after 3 days (or anytime it gets wet). If the ears are standing, leave them alone. If not, tape again. Continue until they remain standing.

Tape the ears individually, or for especially floppy ears, use a bridge of tape between them as well.

you may wish to train him to lie on a grooming table. Make the experience short and pleasant and finish with a treat.

Handle his feet and then eventually use the nail clippers to just tip the smallest bit off the ends of his toenails. The object now is for him to see nail clipping as no big deal. Again, follow with a treat.

Rub your finger along his teeth; then graduate to a soft dog toothbrush. Small dogs tend to have lifelong tooth problems, and brushing his teeth will go far toward preventing them.

Chapter Four

Brains and Beauty

Yorkies are intellectually gifted. They have inquisitive minds waiting to be challenged. A Yorkie mind is a terrible thing to waste.

Training does more than exercise the mind. A well-trained Yorkie is a better companion. She knows how to stay while you leave the door open for a moment, sit politely out of the way while you prepare supper, lie down while you groom her, and come when you call her. Training won't kill your Yorkie's spirit. In fact proper training will nurture it, strengthening the bond between you and your dog by helping your dog understand what you are trying to tell her. When you train your dog the right way, both of you will look forward to spending a special time of learning together.

Training the right way means making learning exciting and rewarding by incorporating play and using lots of toys and treats for rewards. You know how much easier it is for you to learn things that are fun; your dog is no different. She will learn best when her tail is working as fast as her mind. That's why the old-fashioned push, pull, and choke school of dog training was so unsuccessful with Yorkies. They rebel at such treatment. To get a thinking Yorkie to do what you want, it has to be what she wants. One way to do that is with rewards.

Food is a powerful training aid. It is used initially to guide the dog and later as a reward. The dog is then gradually weaned from getting a food reward for each correct response, but instead is rewarded only at random for correct responses. This random payoff is the same psychology used to induce people to put money into slot machines.

You can have it all!

Just because you train with food doesn't mean you are sentenced to carrying a pocket full of dog treats for the rest of your life. As you wean your dog from the food, you substitute less tangible but equally enjoyable rewards, such as praise, petting, or a chance to play with a toy, go for a romp, or play a game.

Run your leash through a piece of PVC pipe for more precise Yorkie level control.

Small Talk
Tools of the Trade

Basic training equipment includes both short (6-foot) and long (about 20-foot) lightweight leads and a collar. Traditionally a slip (choke) collar has been used, but many trainers now prefer a buckle collar for training Yorkies.

A special small dog training tool that some people find handy is a "solid leash," which is a hollow lightweight tube you string your leash through. This helps you guide your dog better when heeling. Otherwise when you pull on the leash it just pulls upward. With the solid leash (and some practice), you can direct the pull in one direction or another. Some dogs are skittish about a stick that seems to hover over their head, so it isn't ideal for all Yorkies.

Another small dog tool is a lightweight stick that you can use to point to where you want your Yorkie to face. You do this by giving your dog a bit of food when she touches the end of the stick with her nose. Some people start with a long spoon with some squeeze cheese on the end of it. Then, after she has the hang of that, you can guide her nose (along with the rest of her body, which must follow) by moving the stick. Other trainers prefer to use the stick as an extension for their own hands, so that they can gently tap (not hit!) or guide the dog into position without bending over every time.

A Yorkie that stays on command makes a great model.

The Click Is the Trick

Clicker training is an effective training technique that's been used for decades to train performance animals, especially dolphins. It works just as well for dogs. In clicker training, you teach the dog that the sound of the clicker (a device available from most pet stores and catalogs) signals that a reward is coming. A clicker signal is used because it is fast, noticeable, and something the dog otherwise does not encounter in everyday life. You can substitute another novel sound. After the dog associates the click with an upcoming reward, you wait for the dog to do the behavior you want. The instant she does so, you click to tell her that her behavior is going to pay off. If she makes a mistake, nothing happens. You just wait for her to do it right, giving her guidance when possible. In essence, the dog thinks she's training you because she realizes that whenever she does a certain behavior, she makes you click and then reward her.

Timing: Timing is important in any training, but especially in clicker training. The crux of training is anticipation: the dog comes to anticipate that, after hearing a command, she will be rewarded if she does something,

It's not too early to start...

Sitting pretty.

and she will eventually perform this action without further assistance from you. Correct timing goes like this:

1. Name. Alert your dog that your next words are directed toward her by preceding commands with her name.

2. Command. Always the same word in the same tone.

3. Action. Don't simultaneously place the dog into position as you say the command, which negates the predictive value of the command. Instead, give the dog time to assimilate your command; then get her to perform the desired action.

4. Reward. As soon as possible after the dog has performed correctly should come a signal (a click or "Good!") followed by a reward.

The sooner a reward follows an action, the better the association. It's sometimes difficult to reward a dog instantly, though, and that's where the clicker comes in. It tells the dog the reward is coming.

Now let's use the clicker to train our Yorkie, Fergie, to sit. First, we click and then reward Fergie many times so that she realizes that a click means a treat is coming her way. You'll need lots and lots of tiny treats because this step usually takes a while. Next we say "Fergie, sit," and we lure her front up and back by holding a treat above and behind her muzzle. If she jumps up for it, don't give it to her. Only when she bends her rear legs do we click and reward. We do it again, clicking and rewarding for successively closer approximations to sitting. Finally Fergie sits, we click, we treat, Fergie's happy, we're happy. Fergie thinks she's trained us; we think we've trained her. We can use the same concept to teach Fergie to lie down, come, heel, bark, stand on her hind legs, crawl on her belly, roll over, or do anything she naturally does on her own.

Small Talk
Training on High
Teach stationary exercises, like "sit," "down," and "stay," on a raised surface. This gives you a better vantage from which to help your Yorkie learn. It also helps keep your little one from being distracted and taking off to play. Of course, make sure that she can't jump off and hurt herself!

Basic Training

It's never too early or too late to start the education of your Yorkie. With a very young puppy, train for even shorter time periods than you would with an adult. The exercises every Yorkshire Terrier should eventually know are sit, come, stay, down, and heel.

Come: Learning to come when called could save your dog's life. Your Yorkie probably already knows how to come; after all, she comes when she's called for dinner. To ensure that she responds to "Fergie, come" with that same enthusiasm, always associate coming when called with good things. Never have your Yorkie come to you and then scold her for something she's done.

To train your Yorkie to come enthusiastically, have a helper gently restrain Fergie while you back away, enticing her until she is struggling to get to you. Then excitedly call "Fergie, come!" and turn and run away. Your helper should immediately release her. When she catches you give her a special reward. If you are clicker training, you can click while she's still on her way to you. Always keep up a jolly attitude and make her feel lucky to be part of such a wonderful game.

Next let Fergie meander around and, in the midst of her investigations, call, run backwards, and reward her when she runs to you. Again, you can click just as soon as she heads toward you. If she ignores you, attach a light line and give her a very gentle tug to guide her to you.

After a few repetitions, drop the long line, let her mosey around a bit, and then call. If she begins to come, run away and let her chase you as part of the game. If she doesn't come, pick up the line and give a tug; then run away as usual.

As Fergie becomes more reliable, you should begin to practice (still on the long line) in the presence of distractions. Hold onto her leash just in case the distractions prove too enticing.

Some dogs develop a habit of dancing around just out of your reach, considering your futile grabs to be another part of this wonderful game. You can prevent this by requiring Fergie to allow you to hold her by the collar before you click or reward her. Eventually you may add sitting in front of you as part of the game. In an obedience trial, a dog must sit in front of you within touching distance in order to pass the recall exercise.

Stay: Bolting through an open door is a potentially deadly habit. Teach your dog to sit and stay until given the release signal before exiting the car or house.

Have Fergie sit, then say "Stay" in a soothing voice (you can omit the dog's name here because many dogs jump up in anticipation when they hear their names—the opposite of what we want them to do when staying). If she tries to get up or lie down, gently but instantly place her back into position. Work up to a few seconds, give a click, and then reward. Then give her a release word ("OK!") so that she knows she can get up. Next, step out (starting with your right foot) and turn to stand directly in front of your dog while she stays. Use you right foot because when training for heeling, you will step off on your left foot—the foot nearest your dog—so she can use that as a heeling cue. Then step back beside her, click, and reward.

It's tempting to stare into your dog's eyes as if hypnotizing her to stay, but staring is perceived by the

The Heel position.

dog as a threat, intimidating her so that she comes to you in appeasement. Work up to longer times, but don't ask a young puppy to stay longer than 30 seconds. The object is not to push your dog to the limit but to let her succeed. Finally, practice with the dog on lead by the front door or in the car. For a reward, take your dog for a walk.

Down: The down command is especially useful for grooming your Yorkie, allowing her to relax and making the process easier for both of you.

Begin with the dog sitting. Say "Fergie, down"; then move a tidbit below her nose toward the ground. If she reaches down to get it, click and give it to her. Repeat, requiring her to reach farther down (without lifting her rear from the ground) until she has to lower her elbows to the ground. This is easier if the dog is on a raised surface and you lower the tidbit below the level of that surface, so that she is peering over the edge. Don't try to cram her into the down position, which can scare a submissive dog and cause a dominant dog to resist. Practice the down/stay just as you did the sit/stay.

Heel: Make her first steps on a leash a good experience by coaxing her a few steps at a time with food. Use a lightweight lead such as a show lead. When she follows you, click, praise, and reward. In this way, she begins to realize that following you while walking on lead pays off.

Many toy dogs are reluctant to walk on lead. They know all they have to do is plant their rears on the ground and look pitiful, and their people will scoop them up and carry them. Sometimes it is safer to carry a toy dog, but you should accustom her to walking on her own four feet whenever possible. Never drag a reluctant puppy. Give her a goal when she's walking. Walk to the kitchen on lead and feed her a treat. If she's a homebody, walk from the street back to the house. If she's an adventurer, walk around the block or to the park. Never let your dog hit the end of the lead and flip or do anything that could possibly hurt her neck. Some Yorkies are predisposed to tracheal collapse and such rough techniques could precipitate problems.

When your puppy is prancing at your side, it's time to ask a little more of her. Even if you have no intention of teaching a perfect competition "heel," she should know how to walk politely at your side. Have her sit in heel position; that is, on your left side with her neck parallel with your leg. Say, "Fergie, heel," and step off with your left foot. During your first few practice sessions, keep her on a short lead, holding her in heel position and giving her a click of approval—and of course, praise. As she gets the idea, you can let out more lead, clicking and praising and rewarding when she is in heel position. The outdated method of letting a dog lunge to the end of the lead and then snapping her back is unfair to any dog if you haven't first shown her what you expect, and it is dangerous for a Yorkie.

Keep up a brisk pace so that she doesn't have time to sniff and sight-see. Add some about-faces, right and left turns, and changes in speed. You can't expect her to sit every time you stop. Be sure to give the "OK" command before allowing her to sniff, forge, and meander on lead.

Higher Education

Advanced obedience skills are well within reach of Yorkshire Terriers, who often relish the chance to do more active exercises than those involved in basic obedience. You can spice up training by adding some more challenging exercises right from the start.

Several advanced exercises require high and broad jumping. Only use extremely low jumps when working with a puppy. They also require retrieving special obedience dumbbells and gloves, so it's a good idea to get these items now while your Yorkie is more likely to want to carry things in her mouth. Other advanced exercises involve hand signals and scent discrimination. Again, there is no reason to postpone introducing these concepts to your dog. Teach hand signals just as you would voice signals; if your dog already knows voice signals, add hand signals by immediately preceding your standard voice command with a signal.

For scent discrimination, train your dog to sniff out hidden objects with your scent on them. Throw a scented object among several unscented objects that are tied down. Your dog will learn that the articles without your scent can't be picked up. Don't contaminate the other objects with your scent by touching them.

Tricks: It's fun to teach your Yorkie tricks. Use the same concepts you used to teach other exercises.

• Teach "catch" by tossing a tidbit or soft toy in an arc toward your dog's nose. Snatch it off the ground before she can reach it. Eventually she'll realize that to beat you to the bounty she'll have to catch it in mid air!

• Teach "shake hands" to your sitting dog by saying "Fergie, shake" and holding a treat in your closed hand in front of her. Some dogs will pick up a foot to paw at your hand, but for most dogs you need to nudge one leg or lure her head far to one side so that she must lift the leg up on the opposite side. As soon as the paw leaves the ground, click and reward! Then require her to lift it higher and longer.

• Teach "speak" by saying, "Fergie, speak" when your Yorkie is about to bark. Then click and reward. Don't reward barking unless you've first said "speak" or you could create a barking monster!

• Teach "roll over" by starting with your dog on her back. Say "Fergie, roll over" and let her go, luring her to an upright position with a treat. Be consistent in having her roll in one direction. After she's doing that, start with her not quite on her back, but lying a bit on the side opposite of the

Yorkies especially like learning active obedience exercises like jumping.

side she needs to roll toward. Lure her over and reward her. Continue until she is starting in an upright position.

Of course, the best tricks are the ones unique to your dog. If your Yorkie has an endearing behavior, make up a cute command and slip it in when she looks as if she's going to do her trick, and give her a good reward when she does it. It may be the first step to fame!

School Days

Good obedience classes are great aids for training your dog to behave properly at home, in public, and in competition. If you take the plunge into competition, class is a place to celebrate wins, laugh about failures, and work on problems. Obedience trials are held amidst great distrac-

tions. It would be nearly impossible for your dog to pass without having some experience working around other dogs.

Get referrals from other trainers of small dogs and sit in on a class. If the class uses outdated yank and jerk methods, look elsewhere. Dogs progress at a different paces. Some dogs are too excited or nervous at first to concentrate on their lesson and may profit from going more slowly and repeating a class.

Yorkshire Terrors

All the cute tricks, fancy heeling, and impressive obedience titles won't mean much if your Yorkie isn't a well-mannered companion at home. But dogs don't always act like we humans think they should. We

Small Talk
Yorkie Talk

Failure to communicate contributes to many behavior problems. People expect their dogs to understand them, seldom bothering to try to learn the dog's language. By learning to speak your dog's language, you can meet your Yorkie half-way.

• A wagging tail and lowered head upon greeting is a sign of submission.

• A lowered body, tucked rear, urination, and perhaps even rolling over is a sign of extreme submission.

• A yawn is often a sign of nervousness. Drooling and panting can indicate extreme nervousness.

• Exposed teeth, raised hackles, upright posture, stiff-legged gait, and direct stare indicate dominant behavior.

• Elbows on the ground and rear in the air, is the classic "play-bow" position, and is an invitation for a game.

Yorkie body language. Clockwise from upper left: aggression, play invitation, submission, and fear.

sometimes inadvertently create behavior problems because we don't understand how dogs naturally behave and think. We too often incorrectly attribute human motives, such as acting out of spite or looking guilty, to simple dog behaviors. We too often think that punishment will teach the dog a lesson. We too often keep punishing despite the fact that

it's not working. If it didn't work so far, why should we expect it to work by doing it again and again?

Until recently there was little choice of where to turn for advice for dog behavior problems. Well meaning but misguided training advice from friends, breeders, or even veterinarians or dog trainers without a scientific background in dog behavior too often only made things worse. Qualified dog behaviorists will consider both behavioral and medical therapies. As a first step in any serious behavior problem, a thorough veterinary exam should be performed.

Yorkies, like all dogs, can exhibit a variety of behavior problems. The most common complaints about Yorkies are their lack of housetraining, fighting with other household dogs, and barking. Yorkies can also do their share of home destruction—they may be small, but they're industrious—either because of boredom or separation anxiety.

Adult soiling: Yorkies can be difficult to housetrain. No matter how gifted your Yorkie is, she will probably not be reliably housetrained until she is almost a year old—assuming that you've done everything right! It's not uncommon for adults to have lapses, and some adults act as though they've never heard of the concept of going outside. You must start from the beginning, treating such dogs as though they were puppies, restricting their freedom and taking them outside frequently. If you haven't tried crate training as an aid, try it now. Don't expect too much from your Yorkie. While older and thoroughly housebroken dogs may ask to go out, it takes a long time for dogs to learn the concept of alerting you that they need to relieve themselves. If training to use the outdoors is not working, consider training her to use a litter box filled with special dog litter.

If an adult continues to eliminate in the house, or if a formerly housebroken dog begins to soil, a veterinary examination is warranted. You and your veterinarian will need to consider the following possibilities:

• Older dogs may not have the bladder control they had as youngsters; a doggy door is the best solution.

• Older spayed females may dribble urine, especially when sleeping; ask your veterinarian about drug therapies.

• Frequent urination of small amounts (especially if the urine is bloody or dark) may indicate a urinary tract infection that requires veterinary treatment.

• Increased urination can be a sign of kidney disease or diabetes and should be checked by your veterinarian. Never restrict water for these dogs; a doggy door or litter box is a better way to cope.

• A housetrained dog that is forced to have an accident inside may continue to soil the same area. If this happens, deodorize the area with an enzymatic cleaner and keep the dog away from it.

• Male dogs may urine mark inside. Castration, especially if done before marking becomes a habit, usually solves this problem. Dog-deterring odorants available at pet stores may help. Many Yorkie owners use a "belly band," which is a pad that wraps around the dog's waist and absorbs the dog's urine. Belly bands are available from many toy dog accessory vendors.

Home destruction can have several causes.

• Submissive dogs, especially young females, may urinate upon greeting you. Excited greetings, yelling, or looming over the dog makes the situation worse. Submissive urination is usually outgrown as the dog gains more confidence.

• Some dogs defecate or urinate when left alone or placed in a cage. They may be suffering from separation anxiety (page 47). You need to treat separation anxiety and restart cage training. Dogs that suffer from cage claustrophobia but not separation anxiety do better if left loose in a dog-proofed room or X-pen.

Home destruction: One of the joys of living with a Yorkie is the hero's welcome you can expect whenever you return home. That joy is greatly diminished if your home is in shambles when you open the door. Home redecoration usually results from boredom or separation anxiety.

Boredom is more common in young Yorkies. Despite their popular image as lapdogs, Yorkies are energetic, inquisitive dogs. Their bodies may be small, but they still need exercise—and their brains need even more stimulation. Without mental and physical exercise, they will make up their own entertainment while you are away, and that usually involves filling the air with a snowstorm of pillow stuffing or making confetti out of books. The best prevention is a brisk walk, small adventure, challenging obedience lesson, or fun game at least once a day, and more often for younger or more active dogs. A dog agility course is a great mind and body exerciser. A variety of interactive toys, given only when the dog is left alone, can help entertain your dog in your absence.

When adults destroy your home, it's often because they are upset at being alone. They are not destroying out of spite but out of separation anxiety. Being left alone is stressful for most dogs. They become agitated and may try to escape, perhaps thinking they can reunite with you. They usually drool, pant, shake, bark, and claw around doors and windows. Punishing them only increases their anxiety and is counterproductive.

Keeping the dog confined in a cage may save your home, but it seldom deals with the anxiety and may even foster fear of being caged. Dogs may urinate or defecate in their cage, rip up bedding, dig and bite at the cage door, bark, pant, shake, and drool. The same is true of locking them in the bathroom. Many dogs are upset by close confinement and do better if they are kept in a room with baby gates or in an exercise pen.

Treat separation anxiety by leaving the dog alone for very short periods and gradually working to longer periods, never allowing the dog a chance to become anxious. If needed, your veterinarian can prescribe antianxiety medications to help during training. When you return, greet your dog calmly, and then have her perform a simple trick you can praise her for.

Fearful behavior: Yorkies are often too brave for their own good. But sometimes a Yorkie can develop unfounded fears, especially of unfamiliar people, other dogs, and thunderstorms.

Some people erroneously think the best way to deal with a scared dog is to overwhelm her with whatever she's afraid of so she gets used to it. The problem is that the dog is usually so terrified that she never gets over her fear enough to realize the situation is safe. The cardinal rule of working with a fearful dog is to go slowly.

Some people erroneously think that petting and comforting their dog will soothe and reassure her. Such actions only reward the dog for acting scared, and further convinces her that you are scared, as well.

Instead, maintain a jolly attitude and make your dog work for praise. Teach your dog a few simple commands; performing these exercises correctly gives you a reason to praise her and also increases her sense of security because she knows what's expected of her.

In some cases, the dog is petrified at even the lowest level of exposure to whatever she is scared of. You may have to use antianxiety drugs in conjunction with training to calm your dog enough to make progress. This is when you need the advice of a behaviorist.

Thunderstorm phobias are particularly common, especially in older dogs. Unfortunately, once they develop, they are hard to cure. Try to avoid fostering fears; act cheerful, play with your dog, and give her a treat when a thunderstorm strikes. Some dogs cope better if they are taken for a car ride during a storm. If you can get a recording of thunder and play it at a low level, you might be able to condition her to it, but that's not always successful. Sometimes providing a dark den to hide in is the only thing you can do.

Barking: Most people appreciate a Yorkie that barks when somebody comes to the door; few appreciate one that barks at falling leaves. If your dog won't stop barking when you tell her to, distract her with a loud noise of your own. Begin to anticipate when your dog will start barking, distract her, and reward her for quiet behavior. Your Yorkie will be a better watchdog if she barks only when appropriate.

Isolated Yorkies may bark through frustration or as a means of getting attention and alleviating loneliness—even if the attention gained includes punishment. The fault is not theirs; they should never have been submitted to solitary confinement in the first place. The simplest solution is to move the dog's quarters to a less isolated location and let her be part of the family. If barking occurs when you put your dog to bed, move her bed into your bedroom, or condition her by rewarding her for successively longer periods of quiet behavior. The distraction of a special chew toy, given only at bedtime, may help alleviate barking. Remember, a sleeping dog can't bark, so exercise can be a big help.

Biting: Puppies and dogs play with each other by growling and biting. If your Yorkie is an only dog, she will probably play with you the same way. Some people mistake this play for aggression; look for these signs that it's all in good fun:

• Wagging tail
• Down on elbows in front, with the rump in the air (the play-bow position)
• Barks intermingled with growls
• Lying down or rolling over
• Bounding leaps or running in circles
• Mouthing or chewing on you or other objects

Even though your Yorkie is playing, it doesn't mean you should let her gnaw your fingers off. When your puppy bites, you simply say "Ouch! No!" and remove your hand from her mouth. Replace it with a toy. If she doesn't get the message just walk away and ignore her. Slapping her is uncalled for—she was just trying to play and meant no harm. Slapping also is a form of aggression that could give your dog the idea that she had better try harder next time because you're playing the game a lot rougher. You don't want to encourage overzealous play, but you don't want to punish it. You want to redirect it.

Although true aggression toward people is unusual in Yorkies, it can occur. Look for these signs that you'd better watch out:
• Low growl combined with a direct stare
• Tail held stiffly
• Sudden, unpredictable bites
• Growling or biting in defense of food, toys, or bed
• Growling or biting in response to punishment

Unprecedented aggression can sometimes be caused by a medical problem, such as a brain tumor, endocrine problem, or a painful condition. Although these are not common sources of aggression, it's worth having a veterinarian check your Yorkie.

More often aggression results from fear or from confusion over who is the leader. It's easy to coddle and shelter a Yorkie as she's growing up, and sometimes young Yorkies don't get needed socialization around unfamiliar people. When they are forced to interact as adults, they may cringe, try to escape, and, failing that, give a warning growl and even snap in self-defense. If the dog is afraid of people, don't let people push themselves on her. Shy dogs are like shy people: they are not so much afraid of people as they are of being the center of people's attention. Remember that, even though direct eye contact is seen as a sign of sincerity in humans, a dog interprets staring as a threat, and it can further frighten a fearful dog. Strangers should be asked to ignore shy dogs, even when approached by the dog. When the dog gets braver, have the stranger offer her a tidbit, at first while not even looking at the dog. It's a slow but rewarding process. It's not necessary for your dog to love strangers, but she should be comfortable enough with them that she can be professionally groomed, treated by a veterinarian, boarded, or caught if lost, without being emotionally traumatized.

Many Yorkies have king complexes, and many Yorkie owners reinforce their dogs' inflated self perception by waiting on them, letting them have their way, petting them

Coddling a toy dog often leads to behavior problems.

on demand, giving them food on request, and basically acting like their Yorkies' servants. True, most owners are their Yorkie's servants, but the secret is to not allow your Yorkie to realize the extent to which she rules your life. A few Yorkies let things go to their heads and become tyrants; when you do something outrageously insubordinate such as trying to move them so that you can sit in your favorite chair, they let you know you are out of line. Of course, it is the dog who is out of line, and in such cases you must relinquish your servant role. You do this not by physically dominating your dog, but

Your dog is a reflection of her upbringing.

by not jumping at her every demand. If you wish to give her treats or pats, have her earn them first by performing some simple tricks. The message is that you love her but that you call the shots. If she continues to challenge your authority, it may be time for a visit to a certified animal behavior therapist.

No dog, and no owner, is perfect. The only dog guaranteed to behave perfectly is a stuffed one. We work with the dogs we have to make them the best they can be, and we love them regardless because their slight imperfections are part of their appeal—just as they love us despite our imperfections.

Chapter Five

Yorkshire Terrier Nutrition

You do something vitally important for your Yorkie every day, something that affects his health and happiness. You fill his food bowl. Be sure you fill it with something tasty and nutritious.

Unlike you, your Yorkie can't choose his menu—except for what he can beg off you and steal from the cat! His diet usually consists of the same thing day after day, making the diet you choose even more critical. Supplements and treats that would be inconsequential to a large dog can make up a significant portion of a tiny dog's diet, so you must be even more careful about handouts. Fortunately, because Yorkies don't eat much, you can afford to splurge on the very best quality foods, or even make your own from the finest ingredients. Nonetheless, choosing the best diet can be confusing.

The Nature of Nutrition

Yorkies are wolves inside. And while they may not bring down an elk to feast upon, their nutritional needs are best met by a diet that reflects their heritage. That means a diet rich in meat. However, wolves also eat vegetable matter. Neither a wolf nor a Yorkie will thrive on an all-meat diet.

A good rule of thumb is that three or four of the first six ingredients of a dog food should be animal derived. These tend to be tastier and more highly digestible than plant-based ingredients; more highly digestible foods generally mean less stool volume and fewer gas problems.

Meat is high in *protein*, which provides the building blocks for growth and maintenance of bones, muscle, and coat, and in the production of infection-fighting antibodies. Puppies, pregnant, stressed, highly active, or underweight dogs need particularly high levels of high-quality protein. Two foods with identical protein percentages can differ in the nutritional level of protein according to the protein's source. Eggs, followed by meat-derived proteins, are of a higher quality and more highly digestible than plant-derived proteins.

You are what you eat.

Fat is also necessary for good health, providing energy and aiding in the transport of important vitamins. Dogs eating diets containing less than 5 percent dry matter fat may have sparse, dry coats and scaly skin. Too much fat, however, can cause obesity and appetite reduction, creating a deficiency in other nutrients. Obese dogs or dogs with heart problems, pancreatitis, or diarrhea should be fed a low-fat food.

Carbohydrates are a fairly inexpensive source of nutrition, but unless cooked, they may be poorly utilized by the dog's digestive system. Carbohydrates derived from rice are best utilized; those from potato and corn are used far less; and those from wheat, oat, and beans are used even less. Excessive amounts of carbohydrates in the diet can cause diarrhea and flatulence and decreased performance.

Fiber should provide a small percentage of a dog's diet. Too much fiber interferes with digestion and can cause diarrhea or large stool volume. Fiber may play a role in weight reduction by making the dog feel full and by preventing digestibility of some of the other nutrients. Better quality fiber sources include beet pulp and rice bran.

A dog's optimal level of each nutrient will change according to its age, energy requirements, and state of health. Prescription commercial diets and recipes for home-prepared diets are available for dogs with special needs. When comparing commercial food labels, keep in mind that differences in moisture content make it difficult to make direct comparisons between the guaranteed analyses in foods with different moisture content unless you first do some calculations to equate the percentage of dry food matter.

Commercial, Raw, and Home-Prepared Diets

Few subjects can start an argument among serious Yorkie fanciers as fast as the comparative merits of feeding commercial, raw, or home-prepared diets. Wild canids evolved eating a diet consisting largely of raw meat plus the vegetable matter in their prey's stomach. The earliest domesticated dogs subsisted largely on human garbage as well as whatever they could catch or forage themselves. For many centuries domestic dogs ate mostly leftovers, scraps, and bread products. Only in recent decades have commercial foods been available.

Commercial: Proponents of commercial foods point out that these diets have been tested on generations of dogs and meticulously adjusted to provide optimal nutrition. Critics of commercial foods point out that these foods are highly processed, do not resemble a dog's natural diet, are not fresh, and may use ingredients unfit for human consumption.

Any commercial food should state that it meets Association of American Feed Control Officials (AAFCO) requirements demonstrated through feeding trials. Better premium commercial foods often use human-grade ingredients. Commercial foods come in dry, canned, and semi-moist varieties, as well as treats. Dry food (containing about 10 percent moisture) is the most popular, economical, and healthful, but least enticing, form of dog food. It can be especially difficult for dogs with tooth problems to eat large kibble. Dry food loses nutrients as it sits, and the fat content can become rancid, so you should only buy small bags for your small dog. Canned

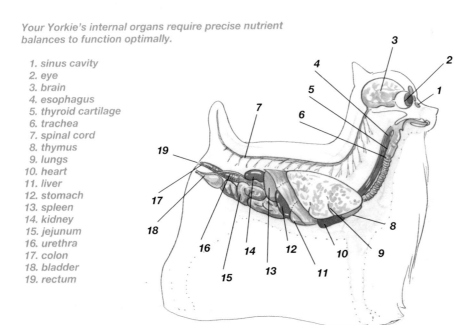

Your Yorkie's internal organs require precise nutrient balances to function optimally.

1. *sinus cavity*
2. *eye*
3. *brain*
4. *esophagus*
5. *thyroid cartilage*
6. *trachea*
7. *spinal cord*
8. *thymus*
9. *lungs*
10. *heart*
11. *liver*
12. *stomach*
13. *spleen*
14. *kidney*
15. *jejunum*
16. *urethra*
17. *colon*
18. *bladder*
19. *rectum*

food has a high moisture content (about 75 percent), which helps to make it tasty. Semimoist foods (with about 30 percent moisture) contain high levels of sugar used as preservatives. Although they are tasty and convenient, they are not an optimal nutritional choice as a regular diet and are especially not suggested as a regular meal in any dog prone to hypoglycemia (see page 32).

Raw: Advocates of raw food diets contend that feeding dogs whole raw animal carcasses or parts more closely resembles the natural diet of ancestral dogs. They claim superior health, clean teeth, and economical food bills. Detractors point out that these carcasses are seldom really whole, having been cleaned of organs and stomach contents. In addition, some people oversimplify these diets, perhaps feeding an exclusive diet of chicken wings, which is neither natural nor balanced. The few controlled studies of the nutritional value of commonly used raw diets have shown most are lacking in important nutrients. Controlled studies on the safety and efficacy of such diets have yet to be published. Critics worry that raw foods from processing plants may pose the threat of *Salmonella* and *E. coli*. Although dogs are more resistant to illness from these bacteria compared to people, they are not immune. If raw food is fed it should be fresh, locally processed, and ground thoroughly, and a legitimate recipe should be followed. Yorkies seem especially poor candidates for these diets. Their jaws

Small Talk
What's in Commercial Dog Food?
• Meat: mammal flesh including muscle, skin, heart, esophagus, and tongue.
• Meat by-products: cleaned mammal organs including kidneys, stomach, intestines, brain, spleen, lungs, and liver, plus blood, bone, and fatty tissue.
• Meat and bone meal: product rendered from processed meat and meat products, not including blood.
• Poultry by-products: cleaned poultry organs, plus feet and heads.
• Poultry by-products meal: product rendered from processed poultry by-products.
• Fish meal: dried ground fish.
• Beef tallow: fat.
• Soybean meal: by-product of soybean oil.
• Corn meal: ground entire corn kernels.
• Corn gluten meal: dried residue after the removal of bran, germ, and starch from corn.
• Brewer's rice: fragmented rice kernels separated from milled rice.
• Cereal food fines: small particles of human breakfast cereals.
• Beet pulp: dried residue from sugar beets, added for fiber.
• Peanut hulls: ground peanut shells, added for fiber.
• BHA, BHT, ethoxyquin, sodium nitrate, tocopherols: preservatives. Of these, the tocopherols are generally considered to present the fewest health risks, but they also have the shortest shelf life.

Dogs are carnivores, but need more than meat in their diets.

may not be capable of chewing bones thoroughly, and their small digestive tracts are more likely to become impacted with bone fragments. Their small bodies are more likely to be severely compromised if they should contract a disease.

Home-prepared: Home-prepared diets from recipes developed by canine nutritionists can include cooked meats and fresh foods and supplements to meet optimal nutrition standards for dogs, but they are more labor intensive than other choices. Do not try to devise such a recipe yourself; canine nutrition is not the same as human nutrition, and the chance of you cooking up a balanced diet is slim. Ask your veterinarian to suggest a reputable source for home-prepared recipes.

Variety: It is a tribute to the dog's general hardiness that most dogs survive under any of these feeding schemes. But for your Yorkie to thrive, you may have to do some experimenting. Varying a dog's diet can provide some insurance that it's getting proper nutrition by providing a wide range of ingredients. In fact, most dogs tend to prefer a novel food, but then tire of it within a few days. The problem is that many dogs develop diarrhea at abrupt changes in diet, so you must change foods gradually with most dogs.

Right on Time

Traditional dog dogma contends that adult dogs should only be fed once a day. This is not good advice for Yorkshire Terriers. Many Yorkies are prone to hypoglycemia, and the best prevention for this dangerous condition is frequent small meals. Very young puppies should be fed at least five times a day, on a regular schedule. Feed them as much as they care to eat in about 15 minutes. From the age of 3 to 6 months, puppies should be fed four times daily, and three times daily until they are about a year old. After that, they should eat twice daily. If you choose to feed more often, make sure that you adjust meal size so that you are not feeding your dog too much.

You may wish to leave food available at all times. This only works with dry food, as most other types will spoil. This method has the advantage that your dog can nibble while you're away but the disadvantage that he may overindulge or, worse, forget to eat when he's busy at play! Forgetting to eat could bring on hypoglycemia in a susceptible dog. The other problem with self-feeding is that you won't realize as quickly when he is off his feed, and so you will miss an early sign of illness.

The Porkie Yorkie

Your dog's weight is the best gauge of how much more or less you should be feeding. All dogs have different metabolisms, so each dog's diet must be adjusted accordingly. The Yorkie is a naturally slender dog with slender limbs. In proper weight, the ribs should be easily felt through a layer of muscle, but they should not feel like a washboard. There should be no roll of fat over the withers or rump, but neither the backbone nor the hipbones should be prominent.

Small Talk
Eating Weird Things
Pica, the ingestion of nonfood items (such as wood, fabric, or soil) can be a problem in some dogs. Talk to your veterinarian about possible health problems that could contribute to these specific hungers and about possible problems that could result from eating these items.

The most common and disturbing nonfood item eaten by dogs is feces. This habit, called coprophagia, has been blamed on boredom, stress, hunger, poor nutrition, and excessively rich nutrition, but none of these has proved a completely satisfactory explanation. Food additives that make the resulting stool less savory are available, and you can also try adding licorice or hot pepper to the stool. A determined dog will not be deterred, and the best cure is immediate removal of all feces. Many puppies experiment with stool eating but grow out of it.

Obesity is not the problem in Yorkies that it is in many tiny breeds, but it does occur. Obesity predisposes dogs to joint injuries and heart problems. Your dog should be checked before embarking on any serious weight reduction effort. Heart disease and some endocrine disorders, such as hypothyroidism or Cushing's disease, or the early stages of diabetes, can cause the appearance of obesity and should

Your Yorkie may think he's people, but he needs dog food, not people food.

be ruled out or treated. A dog in which only the stomach is enlarged is especially suspect and should be examined by a veterinarian.

Chances are your fat Yorkie is simply eating more calories than he is expending. It's hard to deny your friend's pleading eyes on your hamburger and fries, yet it only takes a few morsels to constitute a significant extra meal to a tiny dog. Limit your handouts. Put him in another room when you eat or prepare food. Substitute a low-calorie snack alternative such as rice cakes or carrots. Feed him a lower calorie diet. Commercially available diet foods supply about 15 percent fewer calories per pound and may be comparable to the alternative of feeding less of a fattening food. Research indicates that protein levels should remain moderate to high in reducing diets in order to avoid the loss of muscle tissue. Tasty

low-calorie home-prepared diets are available; ask your veterinarian.

Don't forget the role of exercise. Schedule a walk immediately following your dinner to get your dog's mind off your leftovers—it will be good for both of you.

The Picky Yorkie

A few Yorkies just don't gain weight well, and some are picky eaters. Underweight dogs may gain weight with puppy food; add milk, bouillon, ground beef, canned food, or a small amount of chicken fat and heat slightly to increase aroma and palatability. Milk will cause many dogs to have diarrhea, so try only a little bit at first. Of course, when you start this, you know you're making your picky eater pickier!

A Yorkie that loses weight rapidly or steadily for no apparent reason should have a veterinary exam. Many diseases can cause weight loss. A sick or recuperating dog may have to be coaxed into eating. Cat food or meat baby food are both relished by dogs and may entice a dog without an appetite to eat. Try cooking chicken breasts or other meat, but ask your veterinarian first. Sometimes nauseous dogs prefer cold food.

Water

Water is essential for your dog's health and comfort. Don't just add water to your dog's bowl, which allows algae and bacteria a chance to grow. Empty, scrub, and refill the water bowl daily.

Some people prefer to have their Yorkies drink from water bottles with

Sneaking snacks makes losing weight difficult!

lick tubes. This keeps the facial hair dry and clean and prevents water dripping all over your floor when the dog walks away from the bowl. However, drinking is slower from a bottle compared to a bowl, and many Yorkies tend not to drink as much water from a bottle. This can be problematic in a dog predisposed to urinary stones.

Special Diets

The importance of what you feed is never so noticeable as when your dog has a chronic illness. Several diseases can be adversely affected by feeding some normal dog food ingredients. Commercial diets are available for most major diseases that are influenced by diet, and home-prepared recipes are also available. Because many dogs tire of these diets, owners often supplement these special diets with treats that offset the proper nutrition. Understanding the dietary requirements can help you choose proper foods and treats for an affected dog. Sometimes compromises must be made to ensure your dog a pleasurable mealtime. Any restricted diet should be undertaken only under veterinary advice.

Food allergies: Symptoms of food allergies range from diarrhea to itchy skin and ears. If you suspect that your dog has a food allergy, consult your veterinarian about an elimination diet in which you start with a bland diet consisting of novel ingredients, usually meaning protein sources your dog has never eaten before. Such sources include venison, duck, rabbit, and other unusual foods. Lamb, which is often promoted as hypoallergenic, only fills the bill if your dog hasn't previously eaten it. You may have to keep the dog on this diet for at least a month, withholding treats, chewable pills, and even toys that might be creating an allergic response. If the symptoms go away, then ingredients are added back to the diet gradually. Commercial diets that consist of specially formulated protein molecules that are too small to cause the normal allergic response are available. It may take a lot of experimentation, but a healthy and happy dog will be well worth it.

Feed your Yorkie on a schedule, and don't be late!

Urinary stones: Some Yorkies have a tendency to form calcium oxalate urinary stones. A diet low in oxalate and calcium, with minimal vitamin D, normal phosphorus levels, and high levels of magnesium and citrate is suggested for minimizing this type of stone. These requirements are met by a high-fiber vegetarian-type diet. Your veterinarian can guide you to such a diet that also meets your dog's nutritional needs.

Diabetes mellitus: A diet high in complex carbohydrates, with low fat, moderate protein, and no simple sugars is suggested for diabetic dogs. The feeding schedule is equally important for these dogs. Designing a successful feeding regime for a diabetic dog will require significant commitment and teamwork with your veterinarian.

Liver disease: Dietary management is essential for dogs with liver disease. Of primary importance is that the dog must eat; fasting offers no opportunity for liver damage to recover. Meat should be avoided; preferable protein sources are milk, cottage cheese, or tofu. Simple and complex carbohydrates (such as rice, potatoes, and vegetables) are essential and should be fed in small, frequent meals throughout the day. The addition of fat can increase the meal's tastiness. Vitamin A must be kept to a minimal level, and copper levels must also be kept low.

Pancreatitis: Pancreatitis is more common in older or middle-aged dogs, especially overweight ones. It is often precipitated by a high fat meal, especially from turkey leftovers! Symptoms include lack of appetite,

A prescription diet may help some dogs feel better and live longer.

lethargy, and signs of abdominal discomfort (such as standing with front legs down on the ground in a bowing position), and possibly fever, vomiting, diarrhea, and even shock or death. Although most dogs can eat a high-fat meal without a problem, once a dog develops pancreatitis, a high-fat meal often precipitates subsequent episodes.

Congestive heart failure: A low-sodium diet is the foremost dietary requirement for dogs with congestive heart failure because it reduces blood pressure, in turn reducing the fluid that accumulates in the lungs or abdomen. Some dogs also require slightly higher levels of potassium and magnesium. Because kidney failure often occurs in conjunction with heart failure, finding a palatable diet is often difficult; this, combined with the wasting effect of heart failure and the appetite reducing side effects of some cardiac medications, makes it a challenge to keep adequate weight on these dogs.

Chronic renal disease: Kidney disease is one of the more common problems of older dogs. The role of protein in management of chronic renal disease remains controversial. Protein is necessary to build vital red blood cells, which are deficient in kidney disease. But proteins produce toxic waste products that the kidney cannot clear and that make your dog feel bad. High-quality protein has less toxic waste products. Eggs, beef, and chicken have high-quality protein, although eggs have a high sulfur content that contraindicates their use in dogs with marked acidosis. Reducing phosphorus intake is an essential part of slowing the progression of kidney failure. Salt should be restricted to control hypertension. Designing an appropriate renal diet requires veterinary input and attention to your dog's particular needs.

You are what you eat, and your Yorkie is what you feed him. Choose wisely.

Chapter Six
Crowning Glories

The Yorkshire Terrier wears a cape of quicksilver. It shimmers and flows, undulating about her as she floats across the floor. Such ahhh-inspiring beauty reflects dedication, know-how, and just a little magic.

You have to provide the dedication. Maintaining an opulent coat takes daily attention. This chapter will provide the know-how. You can learn to groom your Yorkie. The magic comes from the special bond between you and your dog that comes from sharing this relaxing activity.

You don't have to aspire to such great lengths. The Yorkie can wear many hairstyles, each delightful in its own way. As long as she is clean and tangle-free, she will radiate charm. In fact, depending on your dog's lifestyle and coat texture, the best thing for her may be a shorter cut. You can preserve the luxurious look of long locks with less labor simply by trimming the coat so that it doesn't touch the floor. Or you can opt for a pixyish puppy cut. Professional pet groomers are well-versed in Yorkie grooming styles and can work with you to find the right style for your dog. You can also learn to do it yourself.

Perhaps you chose a Yorkie because you love the long hair. Take heart; in several ways the Yorkie's hair is easier to live with than the long hair of many other breeds. Because the proper silky coat has no undercoat and doesn't shed, your house won't be covered with hair, and your allergies may react less. Just be aware that

• A long coat requires daily commitment. Skipping coat care for even a few days can undo months of diligence.

• Long body hair can get soiled with urine and feces, and long facial hair with food. They must be washed lest your dog start smelling offensive. A trimmed coat is easier to keep hygienic.

• Long coats can make outdoor activities difficult. They are damaged by burrs, twigs, and grime, and they can become so heavy when wet that they can pull a dog under water.

• A long coat that gets wet, even in places, must be carefully brushed out and dried or it can tangle and mat within hours.

Brushing

Daily brushing and combing is the single most important aspect of Yorkshire Terrier coat care. It's easiest if your Yorkie is trained to lie down on your lap or a table that is slightly higher than lap level for grooming. You'll need a brush, fine- and coarse-toothed combs, and conditioning spray. Use a natural bristle brush because a nylon brush breaks hair. If your dog has a thick or cottony coat, you can also use a pin brush or even a slicker brush, but you must take care not to scratch the dog's skin with them.

Never brush a dry coat. Mist the coat with a spray conditioner or weak mixture of conditioner and water. This protects the coat from breakage and reduces tangle-causing static electricity. Too much conditioner in a silky coat can cause it to appear dirty, however. And although silicone-based products can make brushing and detangling go smoothly, too much silicone can eventually damage the coat.

Brush with the growth of the hair. Don't just brush the surface of the

Perfection.

Small Talk
Grooming Supplies

Many Yorkie grooming supplies can be bought through dog grooming supply catalogs or internet sites (see page 150). You may need the following items:
- Natural bristle brush
- Coarse-tooth comb
- Fine-tooth comb
- Spray bottles
- Coat-conditioning spray
- Corn starch
- Detangling spray
- Shampoo
- Moisturizing conditioner
- Crème rinse
- Blow dryer
- Towels
- Tiny dental rubber bands
- Tiny hair bow
- Hair spray
- Blunt-nosed scissors
- Rice or wax paper
- Knitting needle
- Cotton balls
- Nail clippers
- Tweezers or hemostat
- Electric clipper with several blades
- Mustache trimmer

Make brushing a relaxing time.

coat. Instead, begin at the bottom areas of the dog and lift the upper coat above out of the way. Then brush the coat beginning at its tip and working up the shaft until you're brushing from root to tip. Move up to the next thin layer of coat and repeat until you reach the topmost coat layer. On shorter coats, you can also brush against the growth, and then brush with the coat to get the hair back into the original position.

Tangles: Before moving on to the next layer, use the coarse-toothed comb, followed by the fine-toothed comb, to make sure the section you've been brushing is tangle-free. Tangles can appear even in a carefully watched coat, especially beneath the body, between the front legs, in the armpits, behind the ears, and on the feet. Soft, cottony coats are more prone to tangling than are silky coats. Such coats may profit from a heavier spraying with conditioner, or by using a slicker or pin brush.

Use your fingers to ease out knots. Spraying tangles first with a detangler or silicone, or packing them with cornstarch, may help. Larger tangles or mats may need to be picked apart with a steel comb or a de-matting comb. Pull the hair out of the mat rather than the mat out of the hair. Pull a large mat apart lengthwise and then work on each half. Continue this process until you have several tiny mats. Resist the urge to reach for the scissors. The cut area will look cut and ragged, and may be more prone to mat again.

There are limits. It's no kindness to de-mat an extremely matted dog.

Such a dog is better taken to an experienced groomer who will clip the mats away, allowing the dog to grow a fresh new coat with minimal trauma. The matting may be so close to the skin that it takes an experienced and delicate touch to clip it out without nicking the skin, especially because the skin beneath the area may be so unhealthy that it breaks and bleeds easily. The skin is often already bruised from the constant pulling of the mats as they bunch tighter and tighter with time. After the matting is removed, the area must be bathed gently with a soothing shampoo. The one thing you can't do is ignore mats. They only get worse, binding the dog's movement, inviting skin disease, repelling people, and trapping the

Bad hair days can be scary!

hapless dog in a tattered straight-jacket of hair.

Trimming

All Yorkies need some trimming. You'll need small, blunt-nosed scissors to trim around the ears and feet. You may also wish to get a tiny electric or battery-operated mustache clipper to trim the ears.

Feet: Foot trimming isn't just for appearances; it's also for safety and cleanliness. Hair is slippery, especially on slick flooring, and collects dirt and debris. You want to remove any hair that touches the ground when the dog walks. For a show dog, you would leave an outer drape of hair from the leg. This hair hangs over the foot, forming a column-like appearance. When trimming the foot, it's best to secure the overhanging leg hair up on the leg using a hair clip.

Many Yorkies are ticklish about having their feet touched, so foot trimming takes some patience. One way to do it is to have the dog stand on a grooming table. Pick up the foot opposite of the one you want to trim so that she must leave that foot on the table to stand. Of course, most Yorkies are clever enough to just try to jump in your arms and cute enough to get away with it, but once in while it works for you.

Start by trimming the nails (see page 81). Then trim the foot close, following its contours so that it has a rounded appearance. Next trim the hair from the bottom between the pads. Be careful. Yorkie paw pads are so tiny that it would be possible to snip them off if you used large scissors. Either use small, blunt-nosed scissors, a mustache trimmer, or a clipper with a #40 blade. This blade cuts very close, but lower numbered blades could grab and pinch the pad. No matter what you use, again, be careful.

Ears: The upper third of the Yorkie's ears are trimmed smooth. It's easiest and safest to use mustache trimmers to clip the ears, but you can also use clippers with a #15 blade. Experienced groomers may use a #30 blade for a closer show ring cut, but it's too easy for an inexperienced groomer to nick the fragile ear leather with this blade. Regardless, only clip in the direction of hair growth, never against it. Trim away the hair on the upper third of the front and back of the ear. On the back of the ear, trim the hair so that the shaved area dips down in a V-shape. Then carefully trim the fringe off the edges of the ear leather in the same area, following the contour of the ear. The tip should come to a point. Remember that the leather is very thin here, so be careful not to cut the ear. Ears bleed a lot, so much that you will be sure you've done something horrible, but just apply some styptic powder, or steady pressure, and be more careful the next time.

Anus: You should also trim the hair from around the anus. Use scissors and remove the long hair from

Well trimmed ears allow the hair to frame the face while still appearing alert.

Shave the upper one third of both front and back of the ears, with the shaved area of the back side making a V-shape.

A slightly shorter coat is more practical for outdoor activities.

about a half inch around the anus. This prevents it from getting soiled and avoids unpleasant surprises when holding your dog in your lap! Neglected dogs have been known to be so soiled and matted around the anus that they become impacted or become a hatching ground for flies. These situations require veterinary attention.

While you're at it, carefully trim the hair from around the vulva or penis. This will reduce the tendency for urine to get in the coat, which can cause your dog to smell bad.

Side coat: Even if your dog's coat trails the floor, you still need to trim the ends so that it will look tidy. The best way to do this is to have your dog stand next to the edge of a table on a nonslip surface, so close that her side coat hangs off one end. Comb the hair perfectly straight. Now lift up the outer half of the blue

body coat and use a hairclip to hold it out of the way. This will give access to the hair that grows from the lower half of the body. Trim this hair so that it's even with the feet. Then let the outer layer of the coat down. You want this outer layer to be a little longer and to get gradually longer toward the rear so that it fans out and creates a trainlike effect. Trim it so that it's even with or just below the table until right behind the front legs, and then angle it slightly longer so that it hangs beneath the table. When cutting, smooth each section and use your index and middle finger to hold the coat parallel to your desired cut.

Your Yorkie can have a coat that is much easier to care for, yet still magnificent, if you trim the side coat so that it is about a half inch above the tabletop. This will keep the coat long but off the ground.

For a sportier look, trim the hair in a straight line parallel to the floor and about halfway between the body and floor. This will leave plenty of hair to caress but will give your Yorkie more freedom to cavort in the wilds of your yard.

Companion trims: Most pet owners opt for the short pixie trims that allow maximal freedom from hair worries. You'll need to trim her every 2 to 4 months to maintain the look. You can do it yourself but probably will need to watch somebody with experience do it a few times first. Perhaps your breeder or another Yorkie person can instruct you, or you could pay a professional dog groomer for a lesson. Or you could just have a groomer do the whole job, which is probably the most popular option. If you don't have those choices, you can learn on your own and probably not embarrass your Yorkie too much. The hair will grow back!

Here's a simple way to trim your Yorkie short. You may wish to just clip along the top of the dog, stopping about half way down each side. This will leave the long side coat but it will be thinner and require less care. Or you may wish to continue all the way down and shave it all off.

You'll need electric clippers and a #4, 5, or 8½ blade as well as a #10 blade for them. Many people use a #7 blade instead of the 8½, but the #7 is more likely to cut the skin. Using the #4, 5, or 8½ blade, clip the blue hair of the body in the direction of the hair growth. Your choice of blade will depend on how short you want the hair. The lower the number, the longer the coat it leaves. A #4 blade will leave the coat about 1 or 2 inches long and is used for a true puppy cut. A #5 gives just a bit shorter clip. These lengths are really cute and are also good for colder weather, but they need to be redone more often because they're already fairly long. The #8½ blade will result in a much shorter coat. Trim around the rear with the #10 blade. The #10 blade cuts closer, so if you hate to groom and want the closest possible cut, you could even use it on the body.

On males, trim some of the hair of the abdomen that otherwise gets soiled when he urinates. Or for a closer cut on a male or female, use a #10 blade and cut against the grain throughout the abdominal area up to the rib cage.

You can leave the tan hair of the legs, tail, ears, and rest of the body long or scissor it shorter. It's usually best to trim the tail close.

Use scissors to shorten and shape the facial whiskers to the length you like. For a cute look, begin at the base of the ear and cut the whiskers in a rounded shape around the lower half of the face so that the hair is about 2 or 3 inches long. It will take several tries to get everything even. Then angle back from the dog's nose at about a 45-degree angle, so the hair is shorter near the tip of the muzzle and gets gradually longer farther back.

If you don't want to fuss with a topknot, trim the hair above the eyes in a semicircle from one eye to the other so that the hair sticks up and frames the face. Don't trim the hair just below the eye or on top of the muzzle unless you plan to continue to trim it because when it starts to grow back it sometimes sticks up into the dog's eyes. For a shorter look, use a #10 blade to trim from the outer corner of the eye to the inner corner of the ear. Pull the whiskers forward and clip the neck close, leaving just the longer bottom skirting.

Trim before bathing so that there's less to bathe and dry. But don't put the clippers away just yet. You'll want to tidy up the trim after the bath has rearranged the hair.

Don't expect your first efforts to look professional. There's a reason professional dog groomers are called professionals. But you will get better at it. And your dog won't care.

Bathing

Set aside an hour a week for bathing your Yorkie. You may have to bathe her more often if she gets dirty. Dirt and oil form the foundation of mats, so if you want a long, tangle-free coat, you must keep it clean. Besides natural accumulation of oil from the skin (especially around the ear bases) and dirt from the yard, food can get stuck in the whiskers, fecal matter can get caught in the britches, and urine can soak into the side coat—creating a stew of fragrances making your Yorkie unpleasant to cuddle. You

can postpone bathing by brushing dirt out of the coat and spot washing problem areas. Spot wash using a spritzer bottle with rinse-free shampoo, or dip the hair in a cup of warm water to rinse off regular shampoo.

Preparation: You'll need a good shampoo, conditioner, sponge, towels, and possibly cotton balls and nonmedicated ophthalmic lubricant. The best place to wash your dog is in a sink that has a hand-held sprayer. Place a nonslip pad in the bottom; even a towel will work. You may consider using a leash to hold her in place, but only if you're certain she cannot jump out and hang by it. Even so, never leave her unattended. And make sure that she can't accidentally bump the hot water knob and scald herself.

Before bathing your Yorkie check that she is mat-free. Wetting will make mats draw up and be even more difficult to pry apart afterward. Clean the ears, if necessary, before bathing, as the ear cleanser and debris can be messy. Instructions for ear cleaning are on page 84. Ideally, you can then place cotton balls in the ears to prevent water from getting into them. Realistically, you usually just end up with sopping cotton balls dripping into the ears. You should also place a dollop of clear ophthalmic lubricant in the eyes to protect them from shampoo. Clean the area below the eyes with a cotton ball dipped in warm water. Regardless, you need to take care to keep water and shampoo out of the ears and eyes.

Shampoo: Yorkie groomers can discuss the pros and cons of various shampoos and conditioners for hours. Some contend that any good-quality human shampoo works fine on Yorkie hair because Yorkie hair is similar to human hair. Others point out that human shampoos are made for hair with a pH of 5.5, whereas dog shampoos are formulated for the dog's more alkaline hair with a pH of 7.0. Using a shampoo made for a more acidic hair can dry the hair over time. To complicate matters, the best shampoo depends on your dog's coat type as well as how hard your water is. So you need to experiment, discarding any shampoo that results in dry skin or itching, or that leaves the coat too dry or too oily. It's tempting to judge a shampoo by its suds, but more suds often mean more residue, and more residue means less shine. You may need to use a clarifying shampoo or simply another brand every few washes to remove built-up residue. You may also want to use a human no-tears shampoo around the eyes.

The bath: Begin the bath by wetting your dog down to the skin with warm water. Start at the rear and move toward the head. Holding your dog's ears will often cut down on how often she shakes water all over you. The closer you hold the spray nozzle to her skin—even to the extent of holding it flush to the body—the less she will be tickled and the less she will fling water everywhere. Mix the shampoo with water and then apply it to the coat. Gently distribute

Short trims are practical and cute!

the shampoo all over her body, from the skin down to the tips of the hair. Don't bunch or massage the hair in an overzealous attempt to clean it; you want the hair to survive the bath without breakage or tangling! Let the shampoo do the work. Rinse this initial shampoo, and then do it again. Use a sponge to rinse the face. Be especially thorough with your second rinse to get every bit of shampoo out. Shampoo left in the coat can cause dry hair and itchy skin.

Conditioner or crème rinse: Next apply the conditioner or crème rinse and leave it on for a few minutes. The same dilemmas present themselves

Voila!

when choosing a conditioner or crème rinse as with choosing a shampoo. Human hair conditioners will usually work adequately, but dog conditioners are better suited for dog hair. Crème rinses will give you good immediate, but temporary, results because they coat the hair shaft without treating it. Such products may contain salts, wax, or silicone. Conditioners treat the hair shaft and give better long-term results, especially in dry coats. Whichever you use, rinse it thoroughly, perhaps leaving a little bit in if your dog's coat is dry. A silkier coat requires less conditioner than does a cottony coat.

Drying: Finally, it's time to dry. Squeeze the excess water from the coat without pulling it. Then allow her a good wet dog shake. Wrap her in a towel and pat—don't rub—her to get more water off. Change towels when one gets wet and continue to sop up as much water as possible.

Small Talk
Hair Types

Like people, Yorkies vary in hair type. Unlike many other breeds, the hair type doesn't change appreciably when they are neutered or spayed. Some Yorkies have the ideal lustrous, silky coat that is easy to care for. Others have a coat that tends to be cottony, meaning that it is somewhat dry and puffy. It tends to tangle and break. Such a coat can profit from a coat treatment with a conditioner that restores moisture and protein to the hair. Some Yorkies have a thicker, almost wooly coat. You can use thinning shears to get rid of some of the coat that lies beneath the outermost layer. Do this by thinning the layers that are lowest on the dog, leaving those that grow from near the dog's back untouched. Take a snip or two, then comb everything back in place and look at the results. Then snip some more or move on to another area. This allows those outer layers to lay flatter and relieves you of some coat care without marring your Yorkie's appearance. Cottony or wooly coats may benefit from a light application of a spray conditioner or mink oil. Dedicate a brush to this job; spray the brush and then brush the dog. This will distribute the spray better than just spraying it on the dog.

After you put her down on the floor she's going to want to celebrate by dashing about madly. Sure it's cute, but be sure she can't slip with her wet paws on a slick floor. Also be sure she can't run outside and turn into an instant mudball. And don't let her get chilled. You've wet her to the skin, and she needs you to dry her to the skin. To do this you need a blow dryer, preferably one on a stand so that you have both hands free. Serious Yorkie groomers use forced-air dryers that expel air at high velocity to blow water out of the coat. Most pet owners use a human blow dryer that uses a combination of wind and heat to dry hair. The heat can be damaging to the coat, but probably won't matter unless you're trying to grow show ring hair.

Start by having her stand just in front of the dryer. Once her hair is more damp than wet, have her lie on her side and, just as you would brush her, gently dry the hair in sections from the bottom up. While doing this, brush the hair in the direction it grows. This will encourage the hair to dry flat. If it dries crooked before you get to it, mist it until it's damp and blow-dry it again.

It's tempting to put your dog in a cage and aim the dryer at her through the door. It's also dangerous. Many dogs have overheated and died while being cage-dried when they were left alone for just a minute and then forgotten. Your dog should never be left alone during any grooming procedure.

Topknots

It's important to keep your Yorkie's hair out of her eyes. You can do this by trimming (see page 67), or simply by pulling it back in two ponytails or a single topknot. If you show your Yorkie you'll need plenty of practice putting the hair into a topknot, and even if you don't, it's a fun challenge for a rainy day. You'll need a comb, a long comb handle or a short knitting needle, several tiny dental rubber bands, perhaps a bow, and immense patience. Yorkie exhibitors accustom their dogs to lying with their head on a small pillow or even a rolled towel, enabling the dog to snooze with her head at a more accessible angle.

The basics of a topknot are simple. Gently gather the hair of the forehead that lies in the area between the out-

A knitting needle can be used to gently pull the hair of the topknot outward into a "poof."

Small Talk
Growing Long Hair

A long coat is the culmination of good genes, good health, and good care. Finding the best genes and providing the best nutrition are covered elsewhere (see Chapters 5 and 10.)

• Keep hair clean. Dirt and oil combine to encourage matting.

• Keep external parasites off! A single flea can cause your dog to scratch and chew, breaking off hair. The saliva from the flea could even cause an allergic reaction, which will be devastating to the coat and irritating to your dog.

• Gently brush and comb your dog every day to catch tangles before they become mats. Remove twigs and leaves that can form the nexus of a tangle.

• Keep your dog off carpeting. Strange though it may seem, carpeting is hard on hair. It breaks the coat. Devoted coat growers rip out their rugs and go for tile or hardwood flooring. They even have their dogs sleep on satin sheets!

• Spot clean areas that become soiled with urine, feces, food, or eye mucus. Any organic material left in the coat will rot, destroying the coat along with it.

• Discourage playmates from yanking out each other's hair. Puppies will be puppies, and part of that is pulling each other around by the hair. Fortunately, by the time their coats grow long they've usually moved on to other types of play. When you do spot them attacking each other's coats, give them a toy to play with and try to divert their attention to less destructive games.

• Don't leave a collar on your dog, or if you do, remove it and groom the neck at least twice a day.

• Consider keeping your dog in wraps. This is a method of wrapping and protecting the long hair, freeing your dog to partake in more normal doggy activities.

• Consider having your dog wear special booties on the rear feet so that she doesn't break her hair by scratching.

• Consider keeping a light conditioner in her hair, washing it out and reapplying it every few days.

side corners of the eyes and comb it back over the head between the ears, placing a rubber band near the base to hold it in place. For an added flair, place a little barrette-style clip-on doggy bow along with the rubber band. If you're feeling smug about your abilities you can even make two topknots—one over each eye—similar to those seen in Maltese.

A common mistake is to gather too much hair for the topknot, or to gather hair from too far back on the head. Make sure that hair fringes from the ears are not included as part of the topknot. This would prevent the ears from moving freely and would be uncomfortable for the dog. Also make sure that the rubber band isn't too tight, and that it's not pulling at any snips of hair, which would also be uncomfortable for your dog and could even cause some bald patches! If you've made her eyes look oriental, the topknot is too tight or starts too far down.

A topknot for the show ring is trickier. It seems every exhibitor has a secret technique, but they all begin with clean, dry hair. The hair is either hairsprayed or lightly gelled, allowed to dry, and then brushed. The object is to add some body inside the topknot and make the fine silky hair thicker and more malleable. Gather and comb the hair, making a crisp part extending directly back from the eyes to the blue of the neck coat. Don't band it yet. Instead, working backwards one small section at a time, use a fine-toothed comb to gently tease the hair near its base. Combine the sections and brush the outer layer so it overlays the teased sections, providing a smooth veneer. Hold it in place with a tiny dental rubber band near the top of the head, just in front of the ears. Next use a thin comb handle or knitting needle to reach into the hair in front of the band, deep enough to catch some of the teased area, and pull it down and forward bit by bit until it creates a poofed out area.

Study lots of pictures of show dogs to decide how big and where to place the poof, the rubber band, and the bow. Then compare your

The finished topknot before the bow is added.

dog's conformation and see if you can adjust the topknot to better flatter it. This generally means a smaller poof for a flatter faced dog and a larger poof for a longer faced dog. Of course, for starters, you'll count yourself lucky if the poof is just somewhere near the middle of the head and you haven't poked yourself with the knitting needle. When you have something that doesn't look too aberrant, smooth the rear part of the ponytail down and then lightly spray the whole thing with hair spray. Always cover your dog's eyes when spraying and don't asphyxiate her with the fumes.

After you've congratulated yourself, it's time to move on to the top poof. Top poofs are only for adult Yorkies, as a puppy's hair is not expected to be long enough to do anything but stick straight up from the bottom poof. Tease the hair

1.

2.

3.

4.

5.

6.

immediately above the rubber band just a bit, and smooth the outer layer of hair over it just as you did with the bottom poof. Use a finger to curl the hair backward; then pinch it together with its base. Spray it with hairspray, squeeze it together, and slip a rubber band over both the hair and your fingers so that you can loop the band around the base a couple of times. Blend any hair that did not get caught up in the ponytail into the neck hair behind the right ear.

Besides the effort involved in putting up a show topknot, it takes additional effort to take the topknot down. If you leave the hairspray or gel in the hair it will cause breakage, so you need to wash it out after the

Taming a tousled topknot:
1. *Comb the hair so it is tangle-free and falls naturally.*
2. *Gather the hair from a point between the outer corners of the eyes and the ears. Comb that section straight up.*
3. *Hold the hair in place with a rubber band, making sure none of the ear fringes are caught up in it.*
4. *Use a knitting needle to pucker the hair out in front so it makes a slight poof.*
5. *Gather the hair and fold it back down, holding it in place with another rubber band on top of the first.*
6. *Comb any remaining hair so it falls to the sides and rear. Attach a decorative bow or barrette.*

show. If you can't wash your dog right away, you can apply a coat oil that will dissolve the stiffness somewhat. When you take down any topknot, don't try to pull the rubber band off. You'll end up breaking the hair. Instead use small scissors—suture removers are perfect—to cut the rubber band without cutting any hair.

Those of you familiar with American Kennel Club rules will question the liberal use of hair sprays and gels when the show rules state that the coat should have no foreign substances in it. That means that strictly speaking, no hair spray or gel is allowed on a dog being shown. Yet this is one of those areas that is quietly ignored in many breeds, including Yorkies (at least when it comes to topknots). If you don't use hair spray, it will be difficult to produce a perfect topknot. If you do, a judge will be technically within her rights to excuse you—as well as all the other entrants—from the ring. Use as little as you can to achieve your desired results.

Wrapping

Show dogs don't just lounge around looking regal. They like to run amok just like other dogs. Even though you don't want them to flounder in the mud, you can help them enjoy more real-dog activities by neatly wrapping up their hair to get it out of the way. A dog in wraps may look weird at first, but think of it as an avant-garde hairstyle.

The coat is divided into small sections, each of which has a piece of waxed or rice paper folded around it. If using waxed paper, place the wax side to the outside of the hair. Some people find the paper that doughnuts are served in to be ideal for all but the longest coats. Fold the paper in thirds lengthwise and place a section of coat down the middle, making sure that the end of the hair is within the paper. Fold each side of the paper over the hair to secure it in place. Next, fold the paper with the hair inside upon itself, from two to three times, until it is roughly square-shaped. Place a small rubber band around the middle of the paper. Now the hair is held off the ground and protected in a little paper coat. Move on to the next section and repeat the process. Most Yorkies grow accustomed to wraps and ignore them, but they may try to chew at them at first. You can spray the wraps with a bitter anti-chew spray until the dog gets used to them. Otherwise a dog could chew off the entire wrap with its section of hair!

Just because she looks so cute doesn't mean that you can leave the wraps in forever. You need to check each day to make sure that no mats are starting where the hair meets the mat, and you have to change the wraps every few days. Moisture inside the wraps can rot the hair and do a lot more damage than would no wraps at all.

Finishing Touches

When you remove the wraps, the hair will likely be crimped where it was folded. You need to spritz the crumpled areas and blow them dry while brushing them straight. If you are headed to the show ring, you'll want to go the extra step and use a heated hair straightening iron (available for human hair) or even a small iron. Take extreme care that nothing hot comes into contact with your Yorkie's sensitive skin or inquisitive nose.

You'll also want a perfect part from the back of your Yorkie's head to the base of her tail. Working with small sections at a time, use a knitting needle or rattail comb to part the hair crisply.

Adjust her topknot and bow, comb her hair to blouse out about her, and take a picture—fast! After all, she's a dog under all that glamour, and she'd just as soon be rolling in the muck!

Professional Groomers

Many Yorkie owners prefer to have their dogs professionally groomed. You can drop her off in the morning, spend the day shopping, and pick her up in the afternoon cleaned and coifed. Some groomers even come to your home and groom your dog in a mobile grooming salon. You'll still need to do some maintenance grooming yourself, but by arranging a standing appointment her hair should never get out of hand.

When you bring your dog to the groomer, the groomer will discuss the optimal trim to fit your dog's lifestyle.

The groomer will also examine her for matting. If she's heavily matted, the cost will need to go up to compensate the groomer for the extra time and work involved in de-matting. The groomer may even suggest that you have her clipped down (a procedure called coat removal), which will save you money and the dog trauma. Only an experienced groomer should perform coat removal procedures. In cases of bad matting, you may even need to sign an acknowledgment that the groomer has informed you that the damaged skin below may develop a rash or may itch or peel. The groomer is not trying to be evasive; the unfortunate truth is that there is no perfect way to remove large, long-standing mats.

One of several advantages of having an experienced groomer work on your dog is that the groomer may spot an abnormality you would not. They often notice infected anal sacs, skin disease, abnormal eye discharge, ear problems, or tooth problems that need veterinary attention. True professional groomers are trained to handle dogs safely and comfortably, even old or lame dogs. They understand that many Yorkies have bad knees (luxating patellas, page 95) and position the legs so that the condition isn't aggravated.

The groomer will trim the nails, clean the ears, brush out the coat, and trim the hair first. Then the dog is bathed. During the bath, the groomer may empty the anal sacs (see page 89). After the shampoo and crème rinse, the dog is blow-dried and brushed again. Then the trim is fine-tuned.

Groomers can be found in many places, from home shops to grooming salons to pet superstores. Not all pet groomers are created equal. Grooming dogs is hard work that requires not only skill and experience but also patience and a love of dogs. You're entrusting not just your Yorkie's hair-do to a groomer but also her comfort and safety. Ask your veterinarian or breeder for recommendations.

Ask any prospective groomer for a tour of the facilities. Unless it's also a pet daycare, each dog should be in a clean cage or kennel, separated from the other dogs. Cages should be sanitized between dogs. The groomer will usually require some proof that dogs have been vaccinated. No dog being groomed should be left unsupervised on a grooming table, in a tub, or with a dryer aimed at it. All employees should treat the dogs gently. No groomer should administer any kind of tranquilizer to your dog.

Ask the groomer about her experience, including where or how she learned to groom and how long she's been in business. Experience is extremely important. After all, you could chop up your dog's coat yourself for free. Inexperienced groomers can nick the skin or cause razor burns. Professional groomers have often graduated from dog grooming schools or apprenticed with more experienced groomers. Some continue to attend grooming seminars,

A Yorkshire Terrier with its coat in full wraps.

and a few are even certified by professional grooming associations.

Your Yorkie is the best judge of any groomer. Is she clean, unharmed, and satisfactorily groomed when you pick her up? Does she seem happy around the groomer? Is she confident when she returns for her next visit? Remember, she can't tell you about her day directly. She depends on you to deliver her to a place where she will be treated well. Do your part, and she'll learn to look forward to her special day at the spa.

Whether draped in robes of silver and gold or sheared chic and sleek, a clean and groomed Yorkie feels good about herself and is a pleasure to gaze upon, hold, and caress. Keeping her that way is part of the deal you made when you chose a Yorkshire Terrier. It's a deal that both of you will enjoy keeping.

Chapter Seven

Good Grooming

Good grooming entails more than coat care and can affect your dog's health. Even if you plan to have your Yorkie professionally groomed, you need to do some routine grooming yourself.

Skin Care

Brushing, combing, and bathing give you the chance to examine the condition of the skin. Skin problems can arise from a long list of possible causes including parasites, allergies, bacteria, fungi, and endocrine disorders.

Your nose can also alert you to skin problems. Nobody wants to cuddle with a smelly Yorkie, but don't just push him off your lap and ignore the real source. Generalized bad odor can indicate a skin problem, such as seborrhea. A far too common cause is smelly saliva from bad teeth; the dog licks himself and the entire dog then smells. Impacted anal sacs can also contribute to bad odor. Check the mouth, ears, feet, anus, and genitals for infection.

Pyoderma, with pus-filled bumps and crusting, is a common skin disease. Impetigo is characterized by such bumps and crusting most often in the groin area of puppies. Both are treated with antibiotics and antibacterial shampoos.

Skin allergies: Flea allergy dermatitis (FAD) is the most common of all skin problems. When even one flea bites a susceptible dog, the flea's saliva causes an allergic reaction causing intense itching not only in the vicinity of the flea bite, but often all over the dog and especially on its rump, legs, and paws. The dog chews these areas and causes irritation leading to crusted bumps.

Besides FAD, dogs can have food allergies (page 58) or inhalant allergies that cause itchy skin. The main sites of itching are the face, ears, feet, forelegs, armpits, and abdomen. The dog rubs and chews these areas, traumatizing the skin and leading to secondary bacterial infections. Because the feet are so often affected, many people erroneously assume that the dog is allergic to grass or dew. Although such contact allergies do exist, they are far less common than flea, inhalant, or food allergies.

Allergens can be isolated with an intradermal skin test, in which small amounts of various allergen extracts are injected under the skin. The skin is then monitored for localized allergic reactions. Blood tests are less expensive but also less comprehensive than skin testing. Either test should be performed by a veterinarian with training in the field of allergic skin diseases, as the results can be difficult to interpret.

External Parasites

Parasites remain one of the most common causes of skin and coat problems in dogs. Their damage is more than skin deep, however; many external parasites also carry serious, even deadly, systemic diseases.

Fleas: Fleas have long been the bane of dogs, but recent advances have finally put dog owners on the winning side in the fight against fleas. The newer products available from your veterinarian are well worth their initial higher purchase price. It's a lot cheaper to put an expensive product on your dog occasionally than a cheap one on daily.

Traditional flea control products are either less effective or less safe than these newer products. Loading the environment with pesticides is an especially unwise choice with tiny dogs that live so close to the ground. Ultrasonic flea-repelling collars are

Good grooming shows.

both ineffective on fleas and irritating to dogs. Feeding dogs brewer's yeast or garlic doesn't work.

Ticks: Ticks can be found anywhere on the dog but most often burrow around the ears, neck, and chest and between the toes. To remove a tick, use a tissue or tweezers because some diseases can be transmitted to humans. Grasp the tick as close to the skin as possible, and pull slowly and steadily, trying not to leave the head in the dog. Don't squeeze the tick, as this can inject its contents into the dog. Often a bump will remain after the tick is removed, even if you got the head. It will go away with time.

Healthy hair requires healthy skin.

Two newer products for tick control are amitraz collars (tick collars) and fipronil spray or liquid. Neither will keep ticks totally off your dog, but they may discourage them from staying. You should still use your hands to feel for ticks on your dogs whenever you are in a potential tick-infested area.

Mites: Mites are tiny organisms that are in the tick and spider family. Of the many types of mites, only a few typically cause problems in dogs.

Sarcoptes mites cause sarcoptic mange, which causes intense itching, often characterized by scaling of the ear tips, and small bumps and crusts of other affected areas. Most of the lesions are found on the ear tips, abdomen, elbows, and hocks. Treatment requires repeated shampoos or dips of the affected dog, as well as other household pets that are in contact with the infected dog. It is highly contagious, even to humans, and spreads by direct contact. Skin scrapings may reveal the responsible *Sarcoptes scabiei* mite. The presence of just one mite lends a definite

Yorkies may pick up unwelcome passengers when they play outdoors.

diagnosis, but the absence of mites doesn't mean that they aren't present.

Demodex mites cause demodectic mange. Unlike sarcoptic mange, it is not contagious and is not usually itchy. Most cases of demodectic mange appear in puppies, and most consist of only a few patches that often go away by themselves. In some cases, it begins as a diffuse moth-eaten appearance, particularly around the lips and eyes, or on the front legs, or the dog may have many localized spots. These cases may get worse until the dog has generalized demodectic mange. Demodectic mange affecting the feet is also common and can be extremely resistant to treatment. A definite diagnosis with a skin scraping should be performed before beginning treatment and before ending it.

Cheyletialla mites are contagious and cause mild itchiness. They look like small white specks in the dog's hair near the skin. Many flea insecticides also kill these mites, but they are better treated by using special shampoos or dips.

Nail Care

Canine nails evolved to withstand constant running and digging. They grow constantly, and very few Yorkies will subject them to sufficient wear and tear to keep them short. Overly long nails impact on the ground with every step, causing discomfort and eventually splayed feet and lameness; they also snag

Cut the hollow tip of the nail so you avoid the sensitive quick.

on carpet loops and other places, sometimes pulling the nail from its bed or dislocating the toe. If dewclaw nails (the rudimentary "thumbs" on the wrists) are left untrimmed they can get caught on things even more easily and can be ripped out or actually loop around and grow into the dog's leg. You must prevent this by trimming your dog's nails every week or two.

It's easiest to cut the nails using a small nail trimmer; even those for cats work well for Yorkies. Either have the dog lie on his back in your lap or have a helper hold him while you cut the nails. If you hold the feet backward so that he can't see them and so you can see the underside of the nail it may be easier. Viewed from beneath the nail, you will see a solid core culminating in a hollowed nail. Cut the tip up to the core, but not beyond. On occasion you will

Even the most active Yorkie won't wear down her nails.

slip up and cause the nail to bleed. Apply styptic powder to the nail to stop the bleeding. If this is not available, dip the nail in flour or hold it to a wet tea bag. Always end a nail trimming session with a treat.

Dental Care

Toy dogs need extra vigilance in tooth care throughout their lives. They are more prone to tooth problems and tooth loss than are large dogs, probably because their teeth tend to be more crowded and their roots are comparatively shallower.

Dental care starts in puppyhood by getting the puppy used to having its mouth examined and teeth brushed. Start by just rubbing the teeth gently with your finger. When your dog is an adult you can graduate to a small dog toothbrush, which is curved to more easily reach the dog's teeth. Meat-flavored dog toothpaste helps your dog enjoy the process. Brushing your dog's teeth daily is one of the best things you can do for his well-being. Dry food and hard dog biscuits, carrots, rawhide and dental chewies are only minimally helpful at removing plaque. Prescription dog food that will decrease tartar accumulation is available.

Tooth plaque and tartar contribute to bad breath and health problems. If not removed, plaque will attract bacteria and minerals, which will harden into tartar. Plaque can cause infections to form along the gum line and then spread rootward causing irreversible periodontal disease with tissue, bone, and tooth loss. The bacteria may also enter the bloodstream and cause infection in the kidneys and heart valves. Some dogs tend to accumulate plaque more readily than others, and some dogs simply will not cooperate enough to keep their teeth clean. Your dog's teeth may have to be cleaned under anesthesia as often as once or even twice a year if you do not brush them adequately.

Long Yorkie hair can get intertwined around their teeth if they nibble on themselves. This can irritate the gums and may even lead to infection—especially if the dog already has tooth and gum problems.

Small dogs tend to have problems with crowded teeth, which can some-

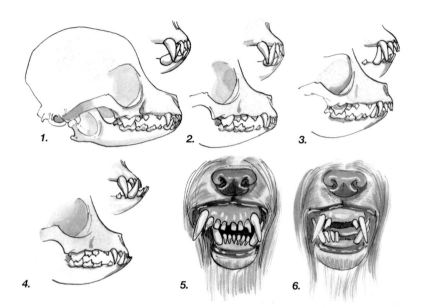

1. 2. 3.

4. 5. 6.

The correct occlusion for a Yorkie is either 1. a scissors (in which the rear surface of the top incisors touch the top of the bottom incisors when the mouth is closed) or 2. level (in which the top and bottom incisors meet each other tip to tip) bite. Incorrect bites include, 3. the overshot bite in which the upper incisors extend beyond the lowers, 4. the undershot bite in which the lower incisors extend beyond the uppers. Other faulty mouths include 5. the wry mouth in which the incisors are uneven or 6. a mouth showing missing teeth.

times displace teeth and affect the occlusion. Correct occlusion is important for good dental health. In correct Yorkshire Terrier occlusion, the top incisors (the little front teeth) should fit snugly in front of the bottom incisors, with the top canines (or fangs) just behind the bottom canines. If the bottom canines are behind or opposed to the top

canines, the bottom ones can be displaced inward and pierce the palate.

Between 4 and 7 months of age, Yorkie puppies will begin to shed their baby teeth. Sometimes the permanent teeth (especially the canines) grow in alongside the baby teeth before they are shed. Because this situation can cause misalignment of adult teeth, some veterinarians advocate removing any baby teeth as soon as it looks like the permanent tooth is coming in or interfering. Because the dog's jaws grow somewhat independently of each other, one of the factors that results in the jaws growing to the same approximate length is the interlock of the teeth. This dental interlock will actually pull or push the teeth of the opposing jaw, and prevent one jaw from growing past the other. This works well in most cases, but if the

A clean dog feels better to herself, and is more pleasant to have around.

Ear Care

The Yorkie's pricked ears allow for good ventilation, helping to prevent many ear problems that flourish in overly moist environments. Unlike in people, the dog's ear canal is made up of an initial long vertical segment that then abruptly angles to run horizontally toward the skull. This configuration makes it difficult to cure ear problems once they have become established. Signs of ear problems include inflammation, discharge, debris, foul odor, pain, scratching, shaking, tilting of the head, or circling to one side. Bacterial and yeast infections, ear mites or ticks, foreign bodies, inhalant allergies, seborrhea, or hypothyroidism are possible underlying problems. Because the ear canal is lined with skin, any skin disorder that affects the dog elsewhere can also strike its ears. Grass awns are a common cause of ear problems in dogs that spend considerable time outdoors. Keep the ear lubricated with mineral oil, and seek veterinary treatment as soon as possible.

jaws do get out of correct position, the teeth can actually prevent them from getting realigned. When this occurs, removal of some baby teeth may help the occlusion improve. It's a good idea to remove teeth only after taking radiographs to make sure that permanent teeth to take their place are below the gumline. Some toy dogs never develop permanent teeth, and when their baby teeth are removed, they are left toothless! Also, be extremely careful that your veterinarian recognizes which teeth are to be removed. Adult Yorkie teeth are so tiny that they are easily mistaken for baby teeth.

If your dog has ear debris, but no signs of discomfort or itching, you can try cleaning the ear yourself, but be forewarned that overzealous cleaning can irritate the skin lining the ear canal and can do more harm than good. If the ear is red, swollen, or painful do not attempt to clean it yourself. Your dog may need to be sedated for cleaning and may have a serious problem. Cleaning solutions will flush debris but will not kill mites or cure infections. Don't stick cotton swabs down in the ear canal, because they can irritate the skin and pack debris into the horizontal canal. Don't use powders in the ear, which can cake, or hydrogen peroxide, which can leave the ear moist.

You can buy products to clean the ear or use a homemade mixture of one part alcohol to two parts white vinegar. Hold the ear near its base and quickly squeeze in the ear cleaner (the slower it drips the more it will tickle). Gently massage the liquid downward and squish it all around. Then stand back and let your dog shake it all out (be sure you're outdoors). If the ear has so much debris that repeated rinses don't clean it right up, you have a problem that will need veterinary attention.

Before rinsing away debris, examine a sample. Ear mites may be visible with a magnifying glass if the material is placed on a contrasting background. The ear mite's signature is a dark, dry, waxy, buildup resembling coffee grounds in the ear canal, usually of both ears. A dog with ear mites will scratch its ears, shake its head, and perhaps hold its head sideways.

Separate a dog with ear mites from other pets and wash your hands after handling its ears. Ideally,

Your Yorkie depends on you to keep his teeth, eyes, and ears clean and healthy.

every pet in a household should be treated. Your veterinarian can provide the best medication. Because ear mites are also found in the dog's fur all over the body, you should also treat the dog's fur with a pyrethrin-based shampoo or spray.

Your grooming efforts will go far to making your Yorkie feel as good as he looks. Make a habit of regularly checking and grooming your Yorkie; you will both be thankful.

Chapter Eight

Medical Matters

Since your Yorkshire Terrier can't tell you where it hurts, you have to be vigilant in watching for signs of illness. Now is the time to get to know what to look for and learn what to do.

Give Your Yorkie the Once-Over

One of the most important parts of home care is being aware of your dog. Watch for signs of lameness, incoordination, balance problems, circling, muscle loss, lethargy, difficulty breathing, coughing, gagging, incontinence, or black or bloody stool. Note changes in behavior, weight, appetite, water consumption, or urination. Listen for soft whining, whimpering, coughing, or wheezing.

Once a week you should give your dog an exam. Start with her mouth. Check her gum color, which should be deep pink. It should also re-pink within a second after you've pressed it with your finger. A longer time can indicate poor circulation. Pale gums can also indicate poor

circulation or anemia. Whitish gums can indicate shock, severe anemia, or internal bleeding. Bluish gums or tongue indicate oxygen deprivation. Bright red gums can indicate carbon monoxide poisoning. Yellowish gums can indicate jaundice. Little tiny red splotches (called petechia) can indicate a blood clotting problem or systemic infection. Don't confuse a red line around the gum line with healthy gums. A dog with dirty teeth can have gum disease, giving a rosy glow to the gum line. Check her teeth to make sure that they are not loose, dirty, or broken. Check her gums and tongue for ulcers, and take note of bad breath.

Next check the rest of her body, including the
• Eyes for mucus, redness, or cloudiness
• Ears for odor, redness, debris, or crusted tips
• Nose for thickened or colored discharge
• Skin for parasites, hair loss, crusts, red spots, growths, or lumps
• Feet for cuts, abrasions, split nails, bumps, or misaligned toes and for foreign objects between the pads

- Anal region for redness, swelling, or fecal matter
- Mammary glands for lumps
- Vulva or penis for discharge

Yorkie Signs and Solutions

One of the difficult problems pet owners are faced with is deciding if their dog is ill. Some common signs that may indicate illness follow.

Lethargy: Lack of energy or interest often signals that your dog isn't feeling well. First check her gum color to make sure her circulation is adequate. If it's not, call the veterinarian immediately.

Fever is another common cause of lethargic behavior. Pain can also cause lethargy, often combined with shivering. Carefully feel all over her body, pressing gently on her limbs, teeth, abdomen, back and neck. Many internal disorders can cause lethargic behavior. The only way to detect them is with professional testing. For example, blood tests may detect problems in many internal organs. Radiographs or ultrasounds may detect internal growths or abnormalities. In most cases, lethargic behavior calls for a trip to the doctor.

Loss of appetite: Loss of appetite often occurs with lethargic behavior, so your first

Gently feel around the area where the rear leg meets the abdomen until you feel the pulse.

Small Talk
Checking the Pulse

To check your dog's pulse, cup your hand around the top of her rear leg and feel around the inside of it, almost where it joins with the torso. You can also feel it directly through her rib cage on her left side, just behind and above her elbow. Normal pulse rate for a Yorkie at rest is about 70 to 120 beats per minute.

steps are to do the same checks you would for lethargy. Try a different diet; like people, dogs sometimes tire of foods. And like people, dogs can develop aversions to foods they ate just before getting nauseous. Usually dogs prefer food that is warmed to body temperature, but nauseous dogs often prefer cold food. So try both warm and cold foods, as well as bland and rich flavors. If your dog continues to have a poor appetite, she needs to see her veterinarian.

Be watchful for changes in behavior or activity.

Small Talk
Body Temperature

Your Yorkie's body temperature is another clue about her health. Lubricate a rectal thermometer and insert it about an inch into her rectum for about 2 minutes, making sure she doesn't sit while it's in. Normal temperature for a Yorkie is about 101 to 102°F. If the temperature is above 103°F, call the veterinarian; over 105°F is an emergency. If it's 98°F or lower, call the veterinarian and begin warming the dog; a temperature of 96°F or lower is an emergency.

Diarrhea: Diarrhea can result from overexcitement or nervousness, a change in diet or water, sensitivity to certain foods, overeating, intestinal parasites, viral or bacterial infections, or ingestion of toxic substances. Bloody or black diarrhea, diarrhea with vomiting, fever, or other signs of toxicity, or a diarrhea that lasts for more than a day requires veterinary attention.

Less severe diarrhea can be treated at home by severely restricting food and water for 24 hours (assuming no other health problems exist). Diarrhea medication is often helpful. You can use one for human babies or children; avoid any containing salt. A bland diet consisting of rice, tapioca, or cooked macaroni, along with cottage cheese or tofu for protein, should be given for several days. The intestinal tract needs time off in order to heal.

Vomiting: Vomiting may or may not indicate a serious problem. Vomiting after eating grass is usually of no great concern, but the following circumstances require veterinary attention:
• Projectile vomiting, or vomit containing blood or anything resembling fecal matter or coffee grounds (which is how partially digested blood looks) could indicate a serious problem.
• Repeated vomiting could indicate that the dog has eaten spoiled food or undigestible objects or has a stomach illness.
• Vomiting immediately after eating could indicate an esophageal problem.

• Sporadic vomiting with poor appetite and generally poor condition could indicate internal parasites or a more serious internal disease.

Coughing: Coughing irritates the throat and can lead to secondary infections if allowed to continue. Allergies, foreign bodies, pneumonia, parasites, fungal infection (especially valley fever), tracheal collapse, tumors, kennel cough, and heart disease can all cause coughing.

Kennel cough is a highly communicable airborne disease caused by several different infectious agents. It is characterized by a gagging cough arising about a week after exposure. Inoculations are available and may be a good idea if you plan to have your dog around other dogs at training classes or while being boarded.

Heart disease can cause coughing, most often following exercise or in the evening. Affected dogs will often lie down and point their nose in the air in order to breathe better. Heart problems leading to congestive heart failure are common in older dogs of any breed. Congenital heart defects occur in dogs of any breed, and Yorkies are no exception. The major such defect in Yorkies is one shared by many breeds, patent ductus arteriosis.

Tracheal collapse is a too-common problem in Yorkies. The trachea, or windpipe, is a flexible tube made of a series of cartilage rings. In some dogs the cartilage isn't as rigid as it should be. Many dogs with abnormal cartilage can live years, perhaps their entire lives, without the condition pro-

Small Talk
Anal Sac Problems

Constant licking of the anus or scooting of the rear along the ground are characteristic signs of anal sac impaction. Dogs have two anal sacs that are normally emptied by rectal pressure during defecation. Their musky-smelling contents may also be forcibly ejected when a dog is extremely frightened. Sometimes they fail to empty properly and become impacted or infected. This is more common in obese dogs, dogs with allergies or seborrhea, and dogs that seldom have firm stools. Impacted sacs cause extreme discomfort and can swell so much that they rupture through the dog's skin. Treatment consists of manually emptying the sacs, sometimes refilling them with an antibiotic ointment and giving the dog oral antibiotics.

Reluctance to get up often signals a problem.

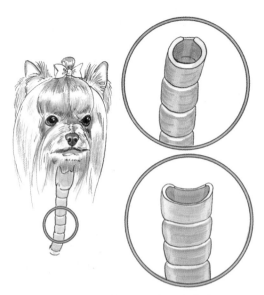

Left: *A normal trachea is rounded, allowing free air flow. Right: A collapsed trachea sags in on itself, blocking airflow.*

gressing to tracheal collapse. Obesity, inhalation of irritants or allergens, respiratory infection, enlarged heart, and endotracheal intubation may precipitate the actual collapse. When the rings collapse, the trachea flattens, obstructing the airway. If the collapse is in the neck region, the dog has problems breathing in; if the collapse is in the chest region, problems are more likely when the dog breathes out or coughs. Coughing further irritates and weakens the trachea, worsening the condition.

Coughing is the major symptom. The cough, a harsh "goose honk" type of sound, occurs mostly during the day and is associated with excitement, pressure to the throat, or eating and drinking. In severe cases, the dog may show symptoms of lack of oxygen, including fainting and a bluish tinge to the gums. Radiographs and ultrasound can be used for an initial diagnosis. However, because the trachea may change its diameter as the dog breathes in and out, a single radiograph may not give an accurate view. That's why it's preferable to use an endoscope to view the trachea directly from within. This procedure often requires a veterinary specialist in internal medicine.

Treatment is usually aimed at controlling symptoms. Weight reduction of obese dogs can be rewarding. Use a harness instead of a collar to lessen pressure on the dog's throat. Humidifying the air, especially in dry climates, is beneficial. The environment should be free of inhaled irritants, especially

Small Talk
Hydration

Repeated vomiting, diarrhea, or overheating can cause dehydration, which can be especially dangerous for a tiny dog. To check your dog's hydration, pick up the skin on her back just above the shoulders, so that it makes a slight tent above the body. It should "snap" back into place almost immediately. If it remains tented and separated from the body, your dog is dehydrated. The most obvious treatment is to give her some water. In severe cases, or in cases in which the dog cannot eat or drink, your veterinarian may need to give her fluids intravenously.

cigarette smoke. Affected dogs should not be stressed, overly excited, or vigorously exercised because panting can cause breathing difficulties. They must be kept free of respiratory diseases. Cough suppressants should be used to reduce irritation to the trachea. The use of bronchodilators is somewhat controversial and is more likely in extreme cases. Glucosamine and vitamin C supplementation may help strengthen cartilage, although their efficacy has not been demonstrated.

In severe cases, surgery to support the trachea using prosthetic supports may be the best option, but it is not always successful. It may be more rewarding in younger dogs and those cases involving the trachea in the neck region. Researchers are still working to develop better procedures, so if you are contemplating surgery, you need to consult with a veterinary surgeon who is abreast of the latest developments in this field, and who has experience with these surgeries.

Tracheal collapse is most common in very small breeds, and it's not known if it's hereditary or a by-product of small size. However, it would seem prudent not to breed a dog with tracheal collapse and to disclose any affected relatives of any dog considered for breeding.

Urinating abnormally: Your dog needs veterinary attention if she has difficulty or pain urinating, urinates suddenly and often but in small amounts, or passes cloudy or bloody urine. Blockage of urine can result in

Many health problems require bed rest—which in turn may require company.

Small Talk
Reverse Sneezing

Don't confuse reverse sneezing—technically called pharyngeal spasms—with tracheal collapse. It looks and sounds alarming, but it is really not a worry. The dog stands with his head thrust forward and front legs spread wide and repeatedly makes long snorting noises. You can try to stop the spasms by getting him to swallow or to breathe through his mouth by rubbing his throat or pinching his nostrils together, but these only work sometimes, and some veterinarians question whether they are really a good practice. Sometimes just distracting the dog with an outdoor diversion will help. The exact cause of reverse sneezing is not known.

Small Talk
Patent Ductus Arteriosis

Patent ductus arteriosis (PDA) is the most common congenital heart defect in all dogs, and Yorkies (especially females) are at an increased risk for it compared to other breeds. PDA occurs when a blood vessel called the ductus arteriosis fails to close after birth. During fetal life, this vessel allows blood to bypass the nonfunctioning lungs; it then normally closes shortly after birth. In some dogs, it remains open, shunting blood to the lungs that should instead be going to the rest of the body. Most puppies with PDA seem completely healthy except for a heart murmur, but some develop heart failure. A definite diagnosis can be made by a veterinary cardiologist using ultrasound, radiographs, and an electrocardiogram.

Although drugs can treat the signs of heart failure, they cannot cure the condition. The best treatment is surgery, preferably by 5 months of age before any permanent damage to the heart occurs. The surgery has a high success rate, and the prognosis is excellent if it's done early enough. Without surgery, most affected dogs die by 2 years of age.

PDA is inherited as a polygenic threshold trait, which means a number of different genes each exerts a small effect until a threshold is reached, at which point the defect occurs. Affected dogs, and even dogs with several affected family members, should not be bred.

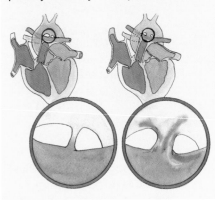

A normal heart (left) compared to a heart with patent ductus arteriosis (right). The large blood vessel (the ductus arteriosis) shunts blood to the lungs that should be going elsewhere.

death. Inability to urinate requires emergency veterinary attention.

Bladder infections must be treated promptly to prevent the infection from reaching the kidneys. In males, infections of the prostate gland can lead to repeated urinary tract infections and even painful defecation.

Dribbling of urine during sleep, most often by spayed females, can indicate a hormonal problem. Kidney disease is one of the most common ailments of older dogs and is marked by increased drinking and urinating. Never restrict water for a dog with kidney disease. Increased urination can also be a sign of diabetes or a urinary tract infection. Your veterinarian can discover the cause with some simple tests, and each of these conditions can be treated.

Uroliths, or stones in the urinary tract, can affect dogs of many breeds, including Yorkies. Several types of uroliths exist. Yorkies are predisposed to calcium oxalate uroliths, which are also the most common type in people. Dogs with calcium oxalate crystals may have underlying metabolic abnormalities that lead to an excess of calcium in the urine; one such cause may be hyperadrenocorticism (see page 139). Excessive amounts of protein, sodium, and vitamin D in the diet, as well as supplemental calcium, promote excess levels of calcium in the urine, but levels may also be affected by some drugs and by a change in intestinal or renal calcium absorption. Dry food diets, as opposed to canned food diets, are also more often associated with urolith formation.

Males are more likely to be adversely affected by uroliths than females because the uroliths can become lodged in the narrow male urethra. This can cause irritation to the urethra, blood in the urine, difficulty urinating, urinating in inappropriate places, and reduced urine stream. Complete blockage can cause kidney failure and death.

A urine sample can often yield crystals, and uroliths can be analyzed to see what type they are. Radiographs or ultrasound may detect stones in the urinary tract. Calcium oxalate uroliths don't respond well to drug or diet therapies, so the recommended treatment usually involves either flushing any stones in the urethra back into the bladder, using shock waves to break them up, or performing surgery to remove them. A special diet containing lower levels of oxalate, protein, and sodium may help prevent their recurrence.

The high incidence of this type of urolith in Yorkies compared to other breeds suggests a genetic connection, although no mode of inheritance has been identified. It is prudent to avoid breeding affected dogs.

Limping: Any time your Yorkie is severely lame, she needs to see her veterinarian. If she is slightly lame, you can try resting her for several days first. If the lameness persists, or if it returns intermittently, she should

Get well soon.

Patellar luxation can make running and jumping difficult.

be checked out thoroughly. Yorkies aren't plagued by large dog problems such as hip dysplasia nor do they seem to be as adversely affected by arthritis. They do have one major worry, which is patellar luxation, as well as a couple of less common problems.

Patellar luxation occurs when the patella, or kneecap, slips out of place. As the knee moves, the patella normally glides up and down along the trochlear groove of the femur (thigh bone). But if that groove is too shallow, or if the quadriceps muscle that helps hold it in place exerts too much rotational pull, the patella can occasionally ride over the ridge of the trochlear groove when the knee moves.

When the patella is out of place (luxated) it usually can't return to its normal position until the quadraceps muscle relaxes, which causes the leg

to straighten at the knee. The dog will often hop for a few steps with its leg held straight forward until the patella pops back into place. As the patella pops over the ridge of the trochlear groove, it may hurt, so some dogs may yelp. Sometimes the patella may not pop back into place on its own. Four grades of patellar luxation severity are described.

• Grade 1: The dog may occasionally skip, holding one hind leg forward for a step or two. The patella usually stays in place unless it is manually shifted out of position. It returns to its correct position easily.

• Grade 2: The dog often holds the affected leg up when running or walking, but the patella usually slides back into position by itself. When the leg is manipulated it has a grinding feeling.

• Grade 3: The patella is permanently out of position. Even when the patella is manually placed back in position, it doesn't stay long. The dog will sometimes use the affected leg.

• Grade 4: The patella is always out of position and cannot be replaced manually. The dog never puts weight on the leg.

Patellar luxation can occur in one or both hind legs, and the patella can be displaced toward the inside or outside. In the Yorkshire Terrier it is almost always displaced toward the inside, which gives the leg a bowed appearance. It's usually present by 4 to 6 months of age, although the symptoms may go unnoticed for several years. It gets gradually worse with age because every time the patella pops out of position it stretches the surrounding tissues that are needed to hold it in place and can even wear down the edge of the trochlear groove. The abnormal wear can lead to arthritic changes, which is one reason it's important to implement treatment early.

You may be able to slow the progress of Grade 1 or 2 luxation by keeping the dog at a trim weight, by building the muscles of the rear with steady, moderate exercise such as walking (especially up hills), and perhaps by giving glucosamine supplements. Surgery to reconstruct the soft tissue surrounding the patella may provide permanent relief if done in these early stages. Many veterinarians consider surgery for Grades 1 or 2, and possibly 3, to be overkill, however, pointing out the discomfort, expense, and possible arthritic aftereffects of such surgery.

Grades 3 and 4 can be quite painful. Surgery may or may not be advised for Grade 3, but is almost always advised for Grade 4. In this procedure, any stretched tissues are tightened and sutured. The groove may be reconstructed if it is too shallow or if its ridge has been worn flat. The quadriceps muscle may need to be realigned if it's pulling excessively on the patella. A veterinary orthopedic surgeon has the special expertise needed to best perform this surgery.

Although the mode of inheritance is unknown, patellar luxation is considered to have a strong hereditary component. Affected dogs should not be bred, and all breeding stock and their close relatives should be checked clear. The Orthopedic Foundation for Animals maintains a

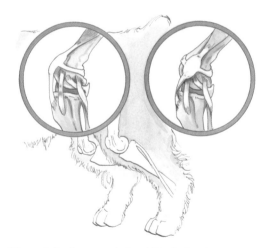

The patella (knee cap) should be in front of the knee (stifle) joint in order to function properly, as shown on the left. When it pops out of the groove that normally holds it there, it is said to be luxated and interferes with proper leg movement, as shown on the right.

Small Talk
Hypoplasia of Dens

The first and second vertebrae (called the atlas and axis bones, respectively) are two large bones of the spinal column situated immediately behind the skull, at the top of the neck. Along the center line of the axis vertebrae is a long projection of bone called the dens, which fits into the middle of the atlas vertebrae somewhat like a peg. This helps secure the two vertebrae relative to one another and prevents substantial up and down movement between them. In some Yorkies, the dens fails to develop properly so it doesn't secure the atlas and axis as tightly as it should. This allows the axis bone to be displaced upward and the spinal cord that runs in a small canal within the axis and atlas to get squeezed. Signs range from pain to paralysis of varying degrees. Treatment is aimed at removing the pressure from the spinal cord by surgically removing parts of the atlas and axis bones and then stabilizing the neck by wiring the two bones together. With surgical intervention the prognosis is excellent.

registry for dogs that have been checked for patellar luxation.

Legg-Calve'-Perthes disease (LCPD) is another condition to which Yorkies are predisposed. The normal blood supply to the head of the femur bone is decreased, causing it to degenerate, weaken, and possibly collapse. This leads to arthritis, pain, poor hip function, and lameness. In most cases, only one leg is affected.

LCPD often starts subtly at 3 to 4 months of age. Radiographs can detect early changes and allow for some preventive measures. Complete and absolute rest of the joint for several months may prevent permanent damage, but this route is difficult with a Yorkie puppy. Placing the leg in a sling was once suggested, but it may cause its own set of permanent problems and is controversial. At present, the preferred treatment is surgical removal of the affected femoral head, followed by physical therapy for several weeks. In small dogs, the muscles are able to hold the joint together adequately even without a femoral head.

A hereditary component is strongly suspected. The best model at present is a single recessive allele with incomplete penetrance. This means that neither affected dogs nor their parents should be bred, and that their siblings may be carriers.

Seizures, stunted growth, and neurological problems: The most common neurological problem in Yorkies is epilepsy, which either occurs for no apparent reason (as it does in many breeds) or subsequent to portosystemic shunting. A couple of other less common problems are occasionally seen, including hydrocephalus. Hypoglycemia causes neurological problems, and is described on page 32.

Portosystemic (liver) shunting is one of the Yorkie's most troublesome breed predispositions. The portal vein takes blood from the gastrointestinal tract to the liver, which removes ammonia from the blood before it reenters circulation. Sometimes side branches emerge from the portal vein and bypass the liver, allowing blood to reenter the circulation without being detoxified. The ammonia in the blood causes neurological problems that may lead to loss of consciousness, bizarre behavior, sudden aggression, seizures, depression, staggering, and sensory problems. It also causes stunted growth and difficulty gaining weight, despite excessive eating (sometimes of bizarre nonfood items). The severity depends on how much blood is shunted around the liver. Signs often start in puppyhood.

Portosystemic shunting may be evident in puppyhood.

A dog that has any of these symptoms, especially a puppy who does not seem to grow or act like its siblings, should have a urine or blood test as an initial screening. A urine test can often detect ammonium biurate crystals, which are typical of portosystemic shunting. Tests of blood ammonia or bile acid concentration, as well as slightly more involved liver function tests, are useful. If the condition is still suspected, an ultrasound or nuclear scan or radiographs taken after a radiopaque dye is injected into the spleen will provide the best information.

Surgery to tie off the aberrant vessels can completely cure an affected dog. However, the surgeon must be experienced because it's vital to adjust the pressure flowing into the liver. If surgery is not an option, a low-protein diet coupled with lactulose to reduce absorption of ammonia can help. If left untreated, the symptoms gradually worsen.

The condition is suspected to have a hereditary basis, and some early evidence indicates that it results from the combined action of several genes. It is prudent to avoid breeding affected dogs as well as the parents of affected dogs.

Hydrocephalus can also cause seizures, as well as slowed learning, incoordination, involuntary movements of the eyes, and visual problems. The brain contains several spaces, or ventricles, that are normally filled with cerebrospinal fluid (CSF). If there is an overproduction or slowed resorption of CSF, the ventricles become overfilled with fluid, exerting pressure on the brain and eventually damaging it.

Hydrocephalic Yorkies may have domed heads with wide-set eyes that look outward toward either side of the head. Although the condition may be evident at birth, more often it is not suspected until the puppy is several weeks, or even months, old.

Diagnostic tests include radiographs, magnetic resonance imaging (MRI), computer-axial tomography (CT) scans, and, if an open fontanel is present, ultrasound. In most cases,

The eyes are the windows to the soul. Keep them clear.

hydrocephalus can be diagnosed by the time a puppy is 4 months of age. Treatment is difficult. Steroids and diuretics may lower CSF levels, but long-term use of these drugs can produce serious side effects. Surgical drainage can have complications and requires that the drainage shunt remain in place permanently. Check with your veterinarian, or even a veterinary neurologist, for updates in treatment options. Depending upon the severity of the particular case, hydrocephalic Yorkies may live long, loving lives.

Shaker syndrome is occasionally seen in Yorkies. Affected dogs will begin to have head and limb tremors that appear over a period of a few days. Treatment is with drug therapy. The hereditary nature is not known, but affected dogs should probably not be bred.

Eye problems: The eyes are the windows to your Yorkie's soul. More importantly, they're the windows to her world. If they get injured or diseased, she could lose her eyesight.

Any time your dog's pupils do not react to light or when one eye reacts differently from another, take her to the veterinarian immediately. It could indicate a serious ocular or neurological problem.

Take note of squinting, redness, itching, tearing, dullness, or mucus discharge. A thick mucus discharge usually indicates an infection or chronic irritation. A clear watery discharge can be a symptom of a foreign body, allergies, or a tear drainage problem. Excessive tearing causes

"Did you say 'needle'? Hide!"

reddish stains on the fur of the face. A clogged or overly small tear drainage duct, which is not uncommon in toy breeds, can cause the tears to drain onto the face rather than the normal drainage through the nose. The eye is a hotbed of hereditary problems in many breeds—and the Yorkie is no exception. Despite what may appear like a long list, eye problems in Yorkies are not as common as they are in many other breeds.

Keratoconjunctivitis sicca (KCS), or dry eye, is a potentially blinding condition that too often goes untreated. It occurs when the lacrimal (tear) glands of the eye produce a reduced amount of tears. Tears are vital for the health of the cornea (the clear outer layer of the eye). When tears are absent or reduced, the cornea not only dries out but also loses the oxygen and nutrients it would normally absorb from the tears. This causes the cornea to become dull looking, and perhaps inflamed, infected, ulcerated, and even opaque. It's an uncomfortable condition, and the eye will often have mucus discharge. KCS is more common in older dogs and in certain breeds, including Yorkshire Terriers. Your veterinarian can diagnose the condition with a simple test.

Sometimes dogs are born with KCS, but more often they acquire it during life from exposure to some drugs and toxins, infections, or injuries. The most common cause, however, is an abnormal immune response in which the body's immune system targets the lacrimal glands and essentially destroys them as it would a foreign invader. Early treatment is important to prevent the condition from worsening and the possible loss of vision.

Small Talk
Blood Tests

Your Yorkie's blood can provide valuable clues about his health. Blood tests are vital before your dog undergoes surgery to ensure that he's healthy enough for the procedure. The most common tests are the Complete Blood Count (CBC) and the Serum Chemistry Profile. Many other specialized tests are fairly common.

The CBC reports:
• Red blood cells: the cells responsible for carrying oxygen throughout the body.
• White blood cells: the infection fighting cells.
• Platelets: components responsible for clotting blood to stop bleeding.

The Serum Chemistry Profile reports:
• Albumin (ALB): reduced levels suggest liver or kidney disease, or parasites.
• Alanine aminotransferase (ALT): elevated levels suggest liver disease.

• Alkaline phosphatase (ALKP): elevated levels can indicate liver disease or Cushing's syndrome.
• Amylase (AMYL): elevated levels suggest pancreatic or kidney disease.
• Blood urea nitrogen (BUN): elevated levels suggest kidney disease.
• Calcium (CA): elevated levels suggest kidney or parathyroid disease or some types of tumors.
• Cholesterol (CHOL): elevated levels suggest liver or kidney disease or several other disorders.
• Creatinine (CREA): elevated levels suggest kidney disease or urinary obstruction.
• Blood Glucose (GLU): low levels can suggest liver disease; high levels can suggest diabetes mellitus.
• Phosphorous (PHOS): elevated levels can suggest kidney disease.
• Total bilirubin (TBIL): level can indicate problems in the bile ducts.
• Total protein (TP): level can indicate problems of the liver, kidney, or gastrointestinal tract.

Treatment begins with identifying the cause, and removing it if possible. Tears can be supplemented with artificial tears or by surgically rerouting salivary ducts to substitute saliva for tears. In dogs with immune-mediated KCS, immunosuppressive drugs may be successful, especially in less-severe cases. The earlier the condition is caught the better the chances for successful treatment; even so, most affected dogs will need life-long treatment.

Corneal dystrophy refers to one of several conditions that affect the opacity of the cornea, the normally clear outer covering of the eye. The type that has been reported in Yorkies, termed subepithelial geographic corneal dystrophy, usually goes away on its own by about 4 months of age.

Be prepared for emergencies, especially on outdoor adventures.

Cataracts are opacities of the lens of the eye. Most people think of cataracts as naturally occurring with age, but many dogs, including Yorkies, sometimes develop them at an early age. Such cataracts, termed juvenile cataracts, are usually inherited. A veterinarian can diagnose the condition by looking in the eye. The only effective treatment is removal of the lens. Juvenile cataracts in Yorkshire Terriers are inherited as a simple recessive. Neither affected dogs nor carriers should be bred.

Progressive retinal atrophy (PRA) is one of the best-known hereditary diseases of dogs, affecting many breeds, including Yorkies. It actually refers to a group of diseases that affect the retina and ultimately cause blindness. In Yorkies, the PRA is late-onset, which means that it affects them only later in life, usually after age 5. Early signs include excessive eye-shine and dilated pupils. A veterinarian can diagnose it. It's inherited as an autosomal recessive.

Prolonged bleeding: Like many other breeds, Yorkies sometimes inherit the most common hereditary blood clotting disorder, von Willebrand's disease (vWD). Several types of vWD exist in dogs, depending on which von Willebrand factor is abnormal. Yorkies are prone to factor VIII deficiency. Its severity varies among affected individuals because of a somewhat randomized factor in the nature of the mutation that causes it. Dogs with only a slight deficiency will have few symptoms, but those with a greater deficiency may have prolonged or uncontrolled bleeding during surgeries or from cuts, lameness from bleeding into the joints, accumulations of blood beneath the skin, or nosebleeds.

A simple blood test is available, but the results have a great deal of fluctuation. About 10 percent of this variability is from variations in the test itself, but most of the variation comes from the dog's variable production of von Willebrand factor. This means that a dog with a suspicious test result should be retested several times before concluding that he is affected.

A dog that also has hypothyroidism is more likely to have a lower von Willebrand factor, so dogs with suspected vWD should be checked for thyroid function. A dog with vWD should be treated with a drug (desmopressin acetate) that increases clotting ability prior to surgery. Although vWD has been reported in Yorkies, it does not appear to be a major problem in the breed. It appears to be inherited as an incomplete dominant, so that dogs with one copy of the abnormal gene will have fewer symptoms than dogs with two copies. A Yorkie shown to definitely have vWD should not be bred.

Small Dog First Aid

The time to prepare for an emergency is now. Have your veterinarian's emergency phone number at hand. Prepare a first aid kit; include a photocopy of emergency numbers and first aid instructions in it. Follow the directions outlined under the specific emergencies, call ahead to the clinic, and then transport the dog to get professional attention.

Your first aid kit should include
• Rectal thermometer
• Scissors
• Tweezers
• Sterile gauze dressings
• Self-adhesive bandage (such as Vet-Wrap)
• Karo syrup
• Instant cold compress
• Anti-diarrhea medication
• Ophthalmic ointment
• Soap
• Antiseptic skin ointment
• Hydrogen peroxide
• Clean sponge
• Pen light
• Syringe (12 cc curved tip is very handy)
• Towel
• First aid instructions
• Veterinarian and emergency clinic numbers

Artificial respiration: If your Yorkie isn't breathing, you may have to give him artificial respiration.

1. Open his mouth, clear the passage of secretions and foreign bodies, and pull the tongue forward.

2. Seal your mouth over the dog's nose and mouth. Blow gently into the dog's nose for 2 seconds and then release. Remember that Yorkies have very small lungs, so don't blow too hard or too long.

3. If you don't see the chest expand, then blow harder, make a tighter seal around the lips, or check for an obstruction.

4. Repeat at a rate of one breath every 4 seconds, stopping every minute to monitor breathing and pulse.

5. If air collects in the stomach, push down just behind the rib cage every few minutes.

CPR: If your Yorkie's heart isn't beating, you should attempt to get it started again with cardiopulmonary resuscitation (CPR).

1. Place your finger tips from both hands, one on top of the other, on the left side of the chest about 1 inch up from and behind the point of the elbow.

2. Press down quickly and release.

3. Compress at a rate of about 100 times per minute.

4. After every 15 compressions, give two breaths through the nose. If you have a partner, the partner can give breaths every two or three compressions.

Seizures: A dog undergoing a seizure may drool, become stiff, or have uncontrollable muscle spasms.

Wrap the dog securely in a blanket to prevent him from injuring himself on furniture or stairs. Remove other dogs from the area (they may attack the convulsing dog). Never put your fingers (or anything else) in a convulsing dog's mouth. Treat the dog for shock. Make note of all characteristics and sequences of seizure activity, which can help to diagnose the cause.

Heatstroke: Early signs of heatstroke include rapid, loud breathing, abundant thick saliva, bright red mucous membranes, and high rectal temperature. Later signs include

unsteadiness, diarrhea, and coma.

Wet the dog down and place him in front of a fan. If this is not possible immerse him in cool water. *Do not plunge the dog in ice water;* the resulting constriction of peripheral blood vessels can make the situation worse. Offer small amounts of water for drinking.

You must lower your dog's body temperature quickly, but you don't want the temperature to go below 100°F. Stop cooling the dog when the rectal temperature reaches 103°F because it will continue to fall.

Even after the dog seems fully recovered, do not allow him to exert himself for at least 3 days after the incident. Hyperthermia can cause lasting effects that can result in death unless the dog is fully recovered.

Hypothermia: Because of their small body size compared to body surface area, Yorkies lose body heat at a faster rate than heavier dogs. This makes them more prone to chilling and hypothermia in cold weather. An excessively chilled dog will shiver and act sluggish. With continued chilling, the body temperature may fall below 95°F, the pulse and breathing rates will slow, and the dog may become comatose.

Warm the dog gradually by wrapping her in a blanket that has been warmed in the dryer. Place plastic milk or soda bottles filled with warm water outside the blankets (not touching the dog). You can also place plastic over the blanket, making sure that the dog's head is not covered. Monitor the temperature. Stop warming when the temperature reaches 101°F. Monitor for shock even after the temperature has returned to normal.

Hypoglycemia: Symptoms of hypoglycemia include drowsiness and incoordination. If the dog is awake, give it food, especially foods containing sugar, to eat. Add Karo syrup if you can get him to eat it. If the dog is unconscious, rub syrup on his gums. For more information about hypoglycemia, see page 32.

Bleeding: Consider wounds to be an emergency if there is profuse bleeding, if they are extremely deep or large, or if they open to the chest cavity, abdominal cavity, or head.

• If possible, elevate the wound site and apply a cold pack to it.

• Do not remove impaled objects; seek immediate veterinary attention.

• Cover the wound with a clean dressing and apply pressure. Don't remove blood-soaked bandages; apply more dressings over them and leave them even after bleeding stops.

• If the wound is on an extremity, apply pressure to the closest pressure point. For a front leg, press inside of the leg just above the elbow; for a rear leg, press inside of the thigh where the femoral artery crosses the thigh bone; for the tail, press the underside of the tail, close to where it joins the body.

• Use a tourniquet only in life-threatening situations and only when all other attempts have failed.

• For abdominal wounds, place a warm, wet sterile dressing over any protruding internal organs and cover with a bandage or towel. Do not attempt to push organs back into the dog.

• For head wounds, apply gentle pressure to control bleeding. Monitor for loss of consciousness or shock and treat accordingly.

• For animal bites, allow some bleeding; then clean the area thoroughly and apply antibiotic ointment. A course of oral antibiotics will probably be necessary. It's best not to suture most animal bites, but a large one (over ½ inch in diameter), or one on the face or other prominent position, may need to be sutured.

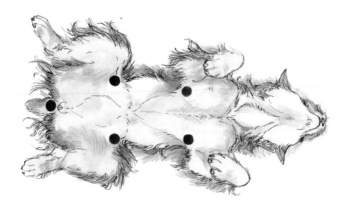

Applying pressure to these pressure points can slow the flow from the large blood vessels that lie beneath them, and help stop bleeding.

Limb fractures: Yorkies have strong legs for their size, but their size nonetheless renders their legs susceptible to fractures. Lameness associated with extreme pain, swelling or deformation of the affected leg, or grinding or popping sounds could indicate a break or another serious problem. Attempts to immobilize fractures with splints tend to do more harm than good, so it's best to keep the dog still and cushion the limb from further trauma without splinting if you can get to the veterinarian right away.

Snakebite: Poisonous snakebites are characterized by swelling, discoloration, pain, fangmarks, restlessness, nausea, and weakness. Most bites are to the head and are difficult to treat with first aid. The best first aid is to keep the dog quiet and to take him to the veterinarian immediately. Antivenin is the treatment of choice, but may not be available. Supportive nursing care including fluid therapy, antibiotics, and anti-inflammatory medications will probably be needed.

Insect stings and allergic reactions: Insects often sting dogs on the face or feet. Remove any visible stingers as quickly as possible by brushing them with a credit card or stiff paper; grasping a stinger often

A vigilant owner is a dog's best protection in an emergency.

your veterinarian beforehand about keeping an antihistamine, such as liquid Benadryl, on hand for such emergencies.

Poisoning

Poisoning is always a concern with dogs. Signs of poisoning commonly include vomiting, convulsions, staggering, and collapse. If in doubt about whether poison was ingested, call the veterinarian anyway.

If the dog has ingested the poison within the past 2 hours and is neither severely depressed, convulsing, or comatose, you may be advised to induce vomiting (unless the poison was an acid, alkali, petroleum product, solvent, cleaner, or tranquilizer). You can do this by giving either hydrogen peroxide (mixed 1:1 with water), salt water, or dry mustard and water.

In other cases, you may be advised to dilute the poison by giving milk, vegetable oil, or egg whites. Activated charcoal can adsorb many toxins. Baking soda or milk of magnesia can be given for ingested acids, and vinegar or lemon juice, for ingested alkalis.

Some all too common poisons are found in the home and garden.
• Ethylene glycol-based antifreeze causes kidney failure; the prognosis is poor after symptoms appear. Veterinary treatment must be obtained within 2 to 4 hours of ingestion of even tiny amounts if the dog's life is to be saved.

Gardens can hide many toxic plants and poisonous substances.

injects more venom into the dog. Administer baking soda and water paste to bee stings and vinegar to wasp stings. Clean the area and apply antibacterial ointment.

Call your veterinarian immediately if you think the dog may be having a severe reaction. Insect stings are the most common cause of extreme allergic reactions in dogs. Swelling around the nose and throat can block the airway. Other possible reactions include restlessness, vomiting, diarrhea, seizures, and collapse. If any of these symptoms occur, immediate veterinary attention will probably be necessary. Ask

- Warfarin-based rodent poisons contain anticoagulants that cause uncontrolled internal bleeding; the prognosis ranges from good (if caught soon after ingestion) to poor (if several days have elapsed).
- Cholecalciferol-based rodent poisons deposit calcium in the blood vessels causing kidney failure and other problems; the prognosis is poor even from eating small amounts.
- Strychnine-based squirrel and bird poisons (usually administered as bird seed with a blue coating of strychnine) can cause seizures, hyperreactivity to noise, and rigid muscles. The prognosis is poor.
- Metaldehyde-based snail and slug poisons cause anxiety, unsteadiness, tremors, coma, and death; the prognosis is fair.
- Arsenic-based insect poisons, weed killers, and wood preservatives cause vomiting, diarrhea, and weakness, progressing to kidney failure, coma, and death; the prognosis is poor if symptoms have already started.
- Organophosphate-based flea and tick poisons and dewormers, in overdose quantities, can cause vomiting, muscle tremors, pupil constriction, diarrhea, excitability, difficulty breathing, and death. The prognosis varies but can be poor.
- Theobromine (found in chocolate and coffee) can cause vomiting, diarrhea, restlessness, fever, seizures, coma, and death; toxic dose for dogs is 50 mg per pound of the dog's weight. Dark chocolate contains over 400 mg of theobromine per ounce of chocolate, so it takes only half an ounce of dark chocolate to be potentially life threatening to a 4-pound dog.
- Lead (found in paint, golf ball coatings, linoleum, and even newsprint) causes abnormal behavior, unsteadiness, seizures, loss of appetite, vomiting, diarrhea, and blindness. The prognosis is usually good.
- Zinc (found in pennies, zinc oxide skin cream, calamine lotion, fertilizers, and shampoos) causes red blood cells to break down. Symptoms include decreased appetite, vomiting, diarrhea, depression, pale gums, and brown urine. The prognosis is variable.
- Iron-based rose fertilizers can cause kidney and liver failure; toxic dose is ¼ teaspoon of 5 percent concentration per 5-pound dog. The prognosis is variable depending upon dosage and treatment delay.
- Onions can destroy red blood cells, especially if large amounts are eaten.

Chapter Nine

Small Victories

Although the best rewards of life with a Yorkie are those you reap simply by sharing everyday experiences, you can add some excitement by venturing into the world of canine competitions. Many people enjoy memorializing the pride they feel for their partner by earning awards and titles or by sharing their dog's love with others.

Little Show-Offs

As you watch the Yorkies at Westminster glide around the ring as if on a cushion of air, it may seem hard to believe that they started out just like yours—more like popcorn in a skillet than seasoned show pros. But even exuberant youngsters have their place in the show scene, and everybody has to start somewhere!

A Yorkshire Terrier conformation show may look like a contest to find the cutest or hairiest dog, but judging is based upon the guidelines in the official breed standard (pages 144–146). Each dog is evaluated on its type (the traits that make a dog recognizable as its breed, including coat, size, proportions, and expression), soundness (the traits that enable a dog to move about as effortlessly and comfortably as possible), and temperament (the traits that allow a dog to coexist happily with people). Evaluating these traits is both an art and a science, and judges must be familiar with dogs in general, as well as Yorkies in particular.

Show training: Champion show Yorkies make their stroll around the show ring look as easy as going for a jaunt in the park. But they're really being gaited at the precise speed that best shows off their movement, and they're being encouraged to display their happy personality without getting out of control. It's not easy to be perfect, but you can work with your Yorkie so that both of you can present a polished look in the ring.

The basics are simple: your dog must learn how to pose without moving his feet and how to trot alongside you—and to do this with confidence amidst the madhouse of a dog show. An upbeat attitude can make your Yorkie stand out from the crowd. Keep him happy so that he doesn't let his tail drop while in the ring and so that he comes to enjoy his time in the spotlight.

Posing: A Yorkie in a show pose stands with legs parallel to each other and perpendicular to the ground, with head and tail up. He must hold this pose while willingly allowing the judge to feel his structure under his coat, looking at his front teeth, ears, legs, feet, tail—and even the testicles (not for the girls, obviously)!

During this individual exam, a Yorkie is posed on an examination table. To place the dog on the table without messing up his grooming, steady his head with your right hand, and place your left hand beneath him from the rear, coming from between his rear legs with your palm supporting his chest between his front legs. You can brush any mussed hairs quickly back in place, but your attention is better spent posing your dog.

At other times, he will pose on the ground, usually with you kneeling beside him. You can teach him to pose by training him with treats or toys to stand attentively in a semblance of the show pose, rewarding him just enough to keep him on his toes. This will keep him in a better mood than will constant posing by hand.

Gaiting: Yorkies are also evaluated on how they trot. Your Yorkie should trot around with his head and tail up. You want him to step out briskly, but at a pace where he doesn't bobble up and down. The lead should be just tight enough that it doesn't droop down, but not so tight that he is hanging from it. Prac-

The multifaceted Yorkie shines in many venues.

tice trotting in a straight line, which is helpful when the judge evaluates his movement from the front and rear.

Practice: You can practice at handling classes, which are often sponsored by local kennel clubs. Obedience classes can be a good place to socialize and practice as long as you let others know you're there to train for conformation. Professional handlers can better groom and present your dog for a fee, but half the excitement is doing it yourself and sharing yet another adventure with your little friend!

At the show: Arrive at the show early so that you can find a suitable place to groom. Allow enough time for you to make a disaster of the topknot a few more times than usual before you get it right.

Carry your dog to ringside in a small cage and keep him there for his protection unless you are actively paying attention to him. Most Yorkie exhibitors carry a Yorkie-sized folding table so that they can do last minute coat touch-ups while keeping the dog out of danger of being stepped on and soiled. Bring a fancy little blanket to drape over the table so that your Yorkie can look especially stunning ringside.

Small Talk
AKC Conformation Classes

AKC shows offer the following classes: Puppy (usually divided into classes for 6 to 9 months and 9 to 12 months), 12 to 18 months, Novice, American Bred, Bred by Exhibitor, and Open. The Best of Breed class is for dogs that are already Champions. All the male (dog) classes are judged before all the female (bitch) classes. Each class winner within a sex competes in the Winners class for points toward the championship title. A dog can win up to 5 points at a show, depending upon how many dogs it defeats. To become an AKC Champion (Ch) a dog must win 15 points including two majors (defeating enough dogs to win 3 to 5 points at a time).

The United Kennel Club also offers conformation competition. Not only are the UKC shows much more relaxed, but they also differ in the classes offered and the requirements for Championships. Unlike AKC shows, at UKC shows you cannot bait or brush your dog in the ring.

Watch the judge's pattern before your class is called. Typically the dogs in each class will enter the ring and pose while the judge looks them over. Then the entire class will trot around the ring once. After that each dog is individually examined on the table and then gaited. Finally, all the dogs are posed in line, and the judge makes his picks. If you're fortunate enough to win a ribbon, take it in stride; if not, congratulate the winner and know that one day you will have the opportunity.

If you make winning the deciding factor as to whether you have fun at a show, you probably won't have a fun day. Only the Best in Show winner remains undefeated at the end of the show, and most people show for decades without ever winning Best in Show. Because your Yorkie is undoubtedly a real member of your family and the apple of your eye, it can hurt to have the judge ignore him. But the judge isn't the one who gets to take him home; you are! And that's the biggest prize of all.

Mind Games

Yorkies may be better known as show dogs, but their quick reactions, merry attitudes, and aptitude for learning make them surprisingly astute obedience competitors. Their obedience ability is surprising because Yorkies don't have a long history of selection for working at their master's direction. Their terrier ancestors were notoriously independent,

Show preparation includes training and grooming.

and their toy influences are more used to having people wait on them than doing their master's bidding. But no Yorkie ever let low expectations get in the way of high performance!

In obedience trials, each dog's performance of a set group of exercises is evaluated against a standard of perfection. One of the most difficult exercises for a tiny dog requires the dog to stand still while the judge examines him, touching him on the head and back. Yorkies also find the "stay" exercises boring and may decide to leave in search of better entertainment. Precision heeling by your side is difficult for tiny dogs. Unlike large dogs that can take their position cues from your torso, Yorkies must either heel while looking up at you instead of where they are stepping or try to cue from your moving lower legs. To look up at your face, it's more comfortable for them to be out from your side. For most exercises, Yorkies must cover the same distance that big dogs cover, which is effectively much longer for them. Tall grass can make some outdoor trials difficult for tiny Yorkies. Smaller Yorkies, compared to larger ones, are at a disadvantage because the distances and jump heights (8 inches) are the same. But since when did a Yorkie let size stand in its way?

Obedience should be fun. You won't pass every trial, so enjoy the

Small Wonders

- The first Yorkie to be credited with an AKC Best in Show (BIS) was Ch Little Sir Model, in 1951.
- Ch Cede Higgins is the only Yorkie to win BIS at America's premier dog show, Westminster. He is also the BIS record holder, with thirty-three such awards.
- In Britain, one of the first Yorkie celebrities was Ch Blairsville Royal Seal, winner of fifty Challenge Certificates (CCs), twelve Best In Shows, and the Top Dog of all breeds in Britain for 2 years. His CC record was broken in 1988 by Ch Ozmilion Dedication, who retired with fifty-two CCs, two Best in Shows, and the Top Dog title. Ch Ozmilion Mystification, winner of fifty-one CCs and Top Dog of all breeds in 1996, gained fame by becoming the only Yorkie to win Best In Show at the prestigious Crufts show.

- Ch Sterling Wild Card O'Marne holds the record for most specialty wins (twenty-eight) in America, including an amazing five national Specialties. He also won three Toy group specialties and fifteen all-breed Best in Shows.
- Ch Glenpetite Sweet Joany is considered the top-winning Yorkie in Australia. She won the Yorkshire Terrier Club of Victoria Championship show an amazing seven times between 1982 and 1989, and Best of Breed at the Melbourne Royal Show an astounding nine times between 1982 and 1991. She received this last award when she was 12 years old, and reportedly was still as stunning as ever.
- Grand Champion Karojenbe Temptation became Australia's first Grand Champion soon after this new title was first offered in the 1990s.

times your dog does something imaginative enough to fail. Those are the stories you'll tell your friends and remember in the years to come.

Canine Good Citizens

Your Yorkie doesn't have to be a scholar to be a well-mannered companion and earn his AKC Canine Good Citizenship title. To do so he should

- Accept a friendly stranger without acting shy or resentful, or breaking position to approach.
- Sit politely for petting by a stranger without acting shy or resentful.
- Allow examination of his ears, feet and coat, along with gentle brushing, by a stranger without acting shy or resentful. He should be clean, groomed, and in reasonably proper weight.
- Walk politely on a loose leash, turning and stopping with you. He need not be perfectly aligned with

Small Talk
AKC Obedience Classes

The AKC offers successively more challenging levels of competition. To earn each title, a dog must qualify at three trials. Each qualifying score requires passing every exercise and earning a total score of at least 170 points out of a possible 200 points.

• Novice is the entry level of AKC competition leading to the Companion Dog (CD) title. Exercises are heeling on-lead and off-lead (sitting automatically each time you stop, making right, left, and about turns, and changing to a faster and slower pace), heeling on-lead in a figure 8 around two people, standing still off-lead 6 feet away from you and allowing a judge to touch him, coming to you when called from 20 feet away, and staying in a sitting position for 1 minute and a down position for 3 minutes with a group of other dogs while you are 20 feet away.

• Open is the intermediate level of AKC competition leading to the Companion Dog Excellent (CDX) title. The dog must heel off-lead (including a figure 8), come when called but drop to a down position when told to do so, retrieve a thrown dumbbell both over a flat surface and over a high jump, jump over a broad jump, and stay in a sitting position for 3 minutes and a down position for 5 minutes with a group of other dogs while you are out of sight.

• Utility is the highest level of AKC competition leading to the Utility Dog (UD) title. To earn a UD, a dog must heel, stay, sit, down, and come in response to hand signals; retrieve both a leather and a metal article scented by the handler from among five other unscented articles; retrieve a glove designated by the handler from among three gloves in different locations; stop and stand while heeling and allow the judge to examine her with the handler standing 10 feet away; trot away from the handler for about 40 feet until told to stop and then turn and sit and then jump over one of two jumps designated by the handler.

• The Utility Dog Excellent (UDX) is awarded to dogs that earn 10 legs in both Open and Utility classes at the same trials after earning the UD.

• The Obedience Trial Champion (OTCh) is awarded to dogs that earn such high scores in Open or Utility that they defeat a large number of dogs. It's the ultimate obedience title.

• Rally Obedience is a less regimented style of obedience in which precision isn't as mandatory. The dog and handler traverse through a course that has signs posted at various places telling them what to do next.

• The United Kennel Club also offers obedience. Its requirements are similar but, in some ways, slightly more challenging. They offer the U-CD, U-CDX, and U-UD.

Waiting ringside.

you, but he shouldn't pull you along.

• Walk on a leash through a group of at least three other people without jumping on them, pulling, or acting overly exuberant, shy, or resentful.

• Sit and lie down on command (you can gently guide him into position) and then stay as you walk 20 feet away and back.

• Stay and then come to you when called from 10 feet away.

• Behave politely to another dog and handler team, showing only causal interest in them.

• React calmly to distractions such as a dropped chair or passing jogger without panicking, barking, or acting aggressively.

• Remain calmly when held by a stranger while you're out of sight for 3 minutes without continually barking, whining, or pacing.

Small Talk
Topknots

Many performance events, including obedience and agility, don't allow dogs to wear anything but a simple buckle or slip collar. An exception is made for certain breeds, including Yorkies, that can wear rubber bands or barrettes to pull their hair back. At the judge's discretion, they may be allowed to wear the same fancy topknot bow they would wear in the show ring.

You can talk to your dog throughout, and precision isn't necessary. Eliminating, growling, snapping, biting, or attempting to attack a person or dog are grounds for failing the test. Bring your dog's buckle or slip collar, brush or comb, leash, and proof of rabies vaccination. All the tests are done on lead; a long line is provided for the stay and recall exercises.

Leaps and Bounds

Maybe their rodent-hunting roots that required them to climb, balance, jump, weave, and run through tunnels make Yorkies so nimble. Despite their small size, they love to challenge an agility obstacle course in a race against the clock. Agility competition combines obedience, athleticism, and most of all, excitement. The AKC, North American Agility Dog Council (NADAC), U.S. Dog Agility Association (USDAA), and UKC sponsor agility trials and award titles. Classes are divided by height, with most Yorkies in AKC competitions competing in the 8-inch jump height class for dogs 10 inches and under at the withers. Some other organizations may require Yorkies to jump a looming 12 inches.

The obstacles are arranged in different configurations from trial to trial. Handlers can give unlimited commands, but they cannot touch the obstacles or dog or use food, toys, whistles, or any other training or guiding devices in the ring. Points

are lost for refusing an obstacle, knocking down a jump, missing a contact zone, taking obstacles out of sequence, and exceeding the allotted time limit. To get a qualifying score, a dog must earn 85 out of a possible 100 points with no non-qualifying deductions.

The obstacles include an A-frame made of two long, wide boards with the peak about 5 feet high, a dog walk made of a long, narrow board suspended about 4 feet high, a see-saw, an open tunnel made of a long, wide, curving tube, a closed tunnel

Posing at Westminster.

Small Talk
AKC Agility Classes

• The Novice class uses between thirteen and fifteen obstacles, including the A-frame, pause table, dog walk, open tunnel, seesaw, closed tunnel, broad jump, panel jump, bar jump, double bar jump, tire jump, and weave poles, plus some additional bar jumps and tunnels.

• The Open class uses between sixteen and eighteen obstacles, including the twelve mandatory obstacles from the Novice class the triple bar jump.

• The Excellent class uses between eighteen and twenty obstacles, including all the Open class obstacles plus additional jumps or tunnels, all in a more complex layout than the lower classes.

For Jumpers With Weaves classes:

• The Novice JWW class uses between thirteen and fifteen obstacles, including one double bar jump, one series of six weave poles, and an assortment of tunnels and bar jumps.

• The Open JWW class uses between sixteen and eighteen obstacles, including one double bar jump, one triple bar jump or broad jump, one series of six to twelve weave poles, and an assortment of tunnels and bar jumps.

• The Excellent JWW class uses between eighteen and twenty obstacles, one double bar jump, one triple bar jump, one series of nine to twelve weave poles, and an assortment of tunnels and bar jumps.

made of a lightweight fabric chute, weave poles, as well as a number of jumps—single, double, and triple bar jumps; solid jump; broad jump; tire jump; and window jump. A pause table on which the dog must sit still for 5 seconds is also included—and is sometimes the biggest challenge for a revved-up Yorkie!

Like any athlete, your Yorkie needs to be conditioned to compete in agility. He should have a health check beforehand to make sure that he's not lame, arthritic, or visually impaired. High jumping and vigorous weaving can impose stresses on immature bones so these trials should be left until adulthood.

Agility with a small dog presents special challenges. The more strides a dog takes between obstacles, the more chances he has to get distracted or turn elsewhere. Handlers must keep up a lively pace but remain close enough to stay in the dog's field of view—not always an easy compromise to make! Obstacles such as weave poles make little sense to tiny dogs because there's so much space between them the dog loses contact with them when weaving. The broad jump, too, has so much space between boards that it seems more sensible to hop between them. The tunnels might seem easy, but they have ridges that can trip a tiny dog.

AKC classes: AKC agility is divided into two types—the Standard agility classes, which include all the obstacles, and Jumpers With Weaves (JWW) agility classes. The latter is a faster paced version of agility that emphasizes jumping and speed without the careful control needed for the pause table and contact points in the Standard agility class. Titles for the Standard agility classes are NA for Novice, OA for Open, AX for Excellent, and MX for Master. JWW titles are the same with a "J" added to the end (NAJ, OAJ, AXJ, and MXJ). The Master Agility Champion (MACH) title is the ultimate designation of superior performance and is obtained by winning 750 championship points and 20 double qualifying scores from the Excellent Standard and Jumpers With Weaves classes.

Hot on the Trail

Your Yorkie's sense of smell enables him to follow a scent laid hours ago, find lost objects, and sniff out contraband. Why not encourage him to use it? The way to train your dog to trail depends upon what motivates him. You can start by walking a simple path and dropping little treats along it. Return to him and help him discover that he can find treats by following your trail. As training progresses, drop the treats farther apart, until eventually only the mother lode of treats is left at the end of the trail. If you have a helper, you can use yourself as the reward, requiring your Yorkie to sniff you out from farther and farther away, until he must follow your trail to jump in your arms.

Small Talk
Small Wonders

• The first Yorkshire Terrier to earn an agility title was U-UD, U-ACH Cupoluv's Magic AbbeeKadabra UD, NA, AD, FDX, CKC-CDX, a feat she accomplished in USDAA, UKC, and AKC venues.

• MACH U-ACHX Herlyn's Funny Girl-Saydie EAC, OJC, NGC earned the first MX and MXJ in AKC agility; she also was the second MACH Yorkie.

• MACH Sunkist Starbright Natasha was the first AKC Master Agility Champion.

• Thompson's Shark With A Bark NADAC Novice Jumpers Certificate, Open Jumpers Certificate, Open Agility Certificate, Novice Gamblers Certificate placed in the top ten in the 8-inch division of the AKC agility Nationals three years in a row.

"Your wish is my command . . . sometimes."

Scent discrimination, one of the exercises in advanced obedience, includes retrieving articles carrying your scent.

Tracking tests once again present special challenges to Yorkies. Distances that aren't taxing to a big dog may be of mammoth proportions to a little dog. High grass, rough terrain, briars, and ditches combined with distances that can be marathon-like to a tiny dog can make following a trail a physical challenge. But at least he doesn't have to bend way down to reach the scent!

Safety First

Yorkshire Terrier owners have the additional concern of safety. Dog shows, obedience trials, and other competitions can be crowded and confusing. Stressed dogs may act unpredictably, and large ones may attack small ones. People are often distracted and fail to pay proper attention to their dogs. Keep your dog in a protective carrier unless you're working with him. When he's out, keep him close and watch for loosely held or aggressive dogs.

Fun and Games

Although conformation, obedience, agility, and tracking are the standard dog competitions, chances are that if a dog can do it, there's a competition for it! Yorkies enjoy dabbling in several additional competitive events.

Dances with dogs: Several organizations sponsor canine musical freestyle competitions, which are

Small Talk
Small Wonders

The first Yorkie TDX is U-CD Illusion's Sarah Ferguson, CD, TDX. "Fergie" is now trying to become the first Yorkie VST.

Small Talk
AKC Tracking Titles

The AKC offers several tracking titles:

• The AKC Tracking Dog (TD) title is earned by following a 440 to 500 yard track with three to five turns laid by a person from 30 minutes to 2 hours before.

• The Tracking Dog Excellent (TDX) title is earned by following an 800 to 1000 yard track with five to seven turns laid 3 to 5 hours earlier. The track crosses a fresher track laid by another person and may traverse various types of terrain and obstacles, including plowed land, woods, streams, bridges, and lightly traveled roads.

• The Variable Surface Tracking (VST) title is earned by following a 3- to 5-hour track, 600 to 800 yards long, over a variety of surfaces such as might be normally encountered when tracking in the real world. At least three different surfaces, including one with vegetation and two without, must be included. Tracks may go through buildings and may be crossed by animal, pedestrian, or vehicular traffic.

• The Champion Tracker (CT) title is earned by a dog passing all three of the tracking tests (TD, TDX, and VST).

competitions in which you and your dog perform a dance-like routine to music. Some competitions emphasize heelwork to music, much like cheek-to-cheek ballroom dancing. Others encourage more intricate and dazzling steps, often at a distance from one another, more like modern dance. Just because you have two left feet is no excuse; your Yorkie has two left feet—and two right ones—and he's willing to give it a spin!

Disc catching: Canine disc-catching contests offer competitions for distance, number of catches in a minute, choreographed trick routines, and accuracy. If they offered ones for cuteness, Yorkies would be unbeatable; as it is, they manage to hold their own.

An agility Yorkie wannabe.

Competing in an agility trial entails lots of jumping.

Of course, don't expect your Yorkie to catch a full size disc. Get a miniature disc, preferably a soft floppy one, which is easier on the teeth. A 6-inch Pocket Pro Frisbee works well for competition. Play fetch with it and then encourage him to run forward, jump up, and grab it out of your hand. After he's doing this enthusiastically, toss it just a couple of inches forward just as he's jumping for it. He will probably be able to snatch it from the air—his first catch! If he misses, beat him to it and then try again. As soon as he understands, you can throw it slightly farther and farther. Have fun, but don't encourage your Yorkie to make leaps that could injure his legs or spine.

The top disc-catching Yorkie, John's Bigger Than a Chigger, faced special challenges when she was competing against the big dogs. Not only did her owner need to convince the organization that a smaller disc size had to be allowed, but the tall grass often slowed her down, even tangling in her hair at times. Throws must be more accurate when dealing with small mouths and small discs.

Flyball: If your Yorkie likes to run, jump, and catch balls, he could have the makings of a flyball contender. Flyball is a relay race in which two teams of four dogs each go head to head down a course of four low hurdles toward a box. The box shoots out a tennis ball when the dog triggers its spring-loaded platform. The dog catches the ball and heads back to the starting line so his teammate can start. The hurdle height is set at 4 inches below the shoulder height of the shortest dog on the team (down to 8-inch hurdles). Teams like having a small dog so that they can have low hurdles. Because this is a team sport, dogs earn points toward titles based on their team's times. Teammates accumulate points toward the Flyball Dog (FD), then the Flyball Dog Excellent (FDX), the Flyball Dog Champion (FDCH), the Flyball Master (FM), the Flyball Master Excellent (FMX), and a couple more titles that no Yorkie has achieved—yet.

Earthdog: Yorkies have always been accomplished rodent catchers, and your Yorkie may still deposit a dead mouse triumphantly in your lap in expectation of praise. So it's no surprise that several Yorkies have jumped at the chance to play earthdog, entering and traversing an underground tunnel until they come face to face with a caged rat, and then barking exuberantly at their find. These are the basic requirements for dogs to earn earthdog titles, which are offered by the AKC and several other organizations to breeds originally bred to hunt underground. But so far Yorkshire Terriers have not been allowed to earn such titles because they lack solid evidence that they historically hunted underground. Perhaps with more Yorkies proving their mettle informally, opinions will change. Meanwhile, you can still go to earthdog trials and practice, and still have fun building tunnels in your yard for your Yorkie to explore.

Therapy Dogs

No doubt your Yorkie is a great comfort to you when you're feeling low. Have you ever considered sharing his love with people who have no furry companions? The shut-in down the street, a shelter for abused women and their children, a nursing home resident, a children's hospital, or a class for challenged children— all are chances for you and your dog to make a real difference in people's lives.

Your visits may range from simply allowing a person to calmly stroke your dog to having your dog perform some tricks for a crowd. A dog is a great way to get the attention of children and to open the door for pet-care education. Yorkies excel as therapy dogs because they greet everyone as though they were dear friends, whether cuddling on a lap or playing a gentle game. Your dog

Small Talk
Small Wonders
The first FDX was probably U-ACH Cupoluv's Magic Abbee-Kadabra UD, NA, AD, FDX, CKC-CDX; the first FDCH was Bear; the first FM was Stimpy the Silver Streak FM; and the first FMX, as well as all-time high-scoring champion, is Madisyn FMX.

Yorkies can do it all. They only need a fair chance.

must be immaculately clean, calm, and trustworthy around new people and in unusual situations. You must do your part and protect your tiny therapist from patients who may not be able to control the force with which they hold or pet your Yorkie.

Although you can do some of these activities informally, you can also join a group that will prepare you and your dog for the situations you'll encounter. They will arrange visits to various facilities and give you the option of going alone, with a friend, or with a group. Your dog can take a course and, upon passing, become a certified therapy dog. Yorkies have touched many lives whether by entertaining, loving, or just sitting in a lap. One of the proudest Yorkies must be "Monk," a service dog specifically trained to help his special person, a young child with cerebral palsy.

Competition provides a world of challenges and adventures for you to share with your Yorkshire Terrier. If you go only to win, you will lose in the long run. If you go to have some fun and make some memories you'll cherish for a lifetime, you'll always be a winner.

Chapter Ten

Breeding Quality

Yorkies are among the loveliest and most beloved of breeds, compelling many Yorkie owners to contemplate producing more of them. Breeding quality Yorkies can be rewarding, but only if you do it the right way.

Breeding by the Numbers

Every hour, ten times more dogs than humans are born in the United States. Many more new dogs than new homes exist. Just because your dog is purebred or AKC registered, its offspring are not guaranteed a good home. More than 25,000 litters producing more than 37,000 Yorkshire Terriers are born and registered with the AKC each year. Do you really think there are 37,000 good new Yorkie homes available each year?

The popularity of Yorkies may seem like one of the reasons in favor of breeding, but it is not. Popular breeds have a difficult time finding good, committed homes; instead, they attract an unusually large percentage of impulse or ill-informed buyers who may be ill suited to own a Yorkie. Popularity also attracts people who have the mistaken belief that they can make money by selling Yorkie puppies. The puppy you unwittingly sell them may live her life as a puppy-making machine, only to be discarded when the entrepreneur discovers how poor a business venture Yorkie breeding really is.

Breeding dogs is good way to lose money. The fact that Yorkies have small litters is an asset in placing puppies, but it makes breeding them financially unrewarding. Sales from a typical litter of three puppies will barely cover expenses if you scrimp, and certainly not cover your investment of time, energy, and worry. If you breed the right way—using the ideal stud, doing prebreeding health screening, and being selective about who you sell to—you'll understand why well-bred Yorkies must command a higher price. Add a caesarean section—an all too common necessity to save the life of the mother and puppies—and you can see why Yorkie breeding can be costly.

Good Homes Come to Good Breeders

Some Yorkies do find good homes, mostly with people who cared enough to do their homework and find good, responsible breeders. In other words, if you want to attract good homes, you need to be a good breeder. Responsible breeders have spent years researching genetics and the breed, breed only the best specimens that have proven themselves in competition, and screen for hereditary defects in order to obtain superior puppies. Unless you have done the same, you are doing yourself,

Breeding your dog is a huge decision.

your dog, the puppies, any buyers, and the breed a great disservice. Remember:

• Unless your Yorkie has proven herself by earning titles and awards, comes from an impeccable background, and has health clearances, you may have a difficult time finding good buyers.

• Breeding toy dogs is not for novices. Risks to the dam and puppies are much greater than risks in larger breeds. Tiny Yorkie females are often too small to carry and whelp a litter and should not be bred.

• Selling puppies will not come close to reimbursing you for the health clearances, stud fee, prenatal care, whelping complications, caesarean sections, supplemental feeding, puppy food, vaccinations, advertising, and a staggering investment of time and energy.

The Perfect Match

If you're still contemplating breeding, do it correctly. Educate yourself about your dog's strengths and weaknesses, get appropriate health clearances (page 11), and become familiar with Yorkshire Terrier lines and studs.

A female worth breeding is worth breeding to the best male available. A worthy stud should have earned titles, which will not only give an impartial evaluation of him but also be helpful in finding good homes. He should also not share the same faults found in your female. Family

Can you assure a happy future for every puppy you produce?

counts; both should come from consistently good backgrounds.

An older (but still fertile) male is preferable, because he has already proven he can live to a healthy old age. Both male and female should pass the same health clearances, not only for genetic health problems but also for communicable diseases including canine brucellosis. Brucellosis causes infertility and can be transmitted through sexual as well as nonsexual contact. Your veterinarian can check for its presence with a blood test.

You should avoid breeding to a male closely related to your female. If you see several names repeated in the proposed pedigree, you may wish to calculate how inbred the resulting puppies would be. The coefficient of inbreeding (COI) refers to the probability that a dog will have identical copies of the same gene that both trace back to a common ancestor. For example, the COI of puppies from a sibling-to-sibling or parent-to-offspring mating is 25 percent; the COI from a mating of a half-brother to half-sister is 12.5 percent. You can calculate this by hand or with some computer pedigree programs.

As a general rule, dogs with low COIs are more likely to be healthy and have long-lived offspring because chances of having two identical recessive genes are less. Most bad genes are recessive, meaning that it takes two identical copies for them to exert their effects on the individual; that's how they lurk in the gene pool.

Potential parents should be sound of body and mind, good representatives of the breed, and complementary to one another.

Breeding and Whelping

Make arrangements with the stud owner well in advance of the breeding. A written contract should spell out what expenses you'll be responsible for and what will happen if no puppies are born. The small litter size of Yorkies often makes it a bad idea to promise a stud fee puppy—you might not be left with one for yourself!

Many Yorkie females are fastidiously clean, and it's easy to miss the first spots of telltale blood. Count the days from the first signs, but don't rely on them to determine the right day to breed. Your veterinarian can pinpoint her ovulation date with a series of blood tests, although many people just leave it to the nose of an experienced stud dog.

Pregnancy determination: Is she pregnant? Human pregnancy tests don't work for dogs, but several signs can give you early clues. Around days 18 to 21 postfertilization, many pregnant females will appear nauseous and even vomit. A canine pregnancy test (Reprochek) can detect the presence of relaxin, a substance produced by the placenta of a pregnant dog after implantation, typically by day 21 to 25 postfertilization. By about day 35, pregnancy can be reliably determined with ultrasound. Other signs that often develop by then are a mucus discharge from the vagina and enlarged, pinkish nipples. If still in doubt, she can be radiographed in her last week of pregnancy, which can also tell you how many puppies to expect.

Gestation: The mother-to-be should be kept active throughout most of her pregnancy, but she should not be allowed to run and jump too vigorously as she nears her whelping date. She should begin to eat more, gradually switching to puppy food during the latter half of her pregnancy. Do not give her supplements without your veterinarian's approval. See page 129 to understand why giving calcium supplements can be dangerous.

Yorkie gestation averages 61 to 63 days from the date of the first breeding, although full-term gestation can range from 57 to 72 days. This variability results from the fact that fertile matings can occur well before and after the actual time of ovulation and fertilization. A more accurate estimate is available if you used ovulation timing during her estrus.

Planned caesarean sections: About 20 percent of Yorkshire Terrier litters must be born by caesarean section. Newborn Yorkies are large compared to the size of their dam, and a large litter often takes up so much room that the dam cannot carry them to full term. Even if she does, the chance of needing a cae-

sarean section are greater because the puppies seem to have difficulty aligning properly in the birth canal. On the other hand, a litter consisting of only one puppy can also be problematic, as the puppy grows unusually large and cannot be whelped naturally; and one puppy may not produce enough of the hormones that play a part in initiating whelping.

Knowing the number and size of puppies before the expected whelping date can help you and your veterinarian decide if a planned caesarean might be the safest choice. If you used ovulation timing during estrus, you can pinpoint the expected whelping date and know the best time to plan a caesarean. Don't compromise on the date just for convenience; with tiny puppies a few days can make a critical difference. Although no one likes putting a tiny dog under anesthesia, caesarean mortality rates are lower for planned caesareans than they are for natural births, and certainly lower than those for unplanned caesareans.

Whelping: Begin taking the expectant mother's temperature

Small Talk
DNA

A simple cheek swab can collect DNA for analysis in cases of pedigree disputes. Litters with more than one sire can even be registered if the DNA from all the puppies and all the potential sires is examined by the AKC.

every morning and evening starting about a week before her due date. When her temperature drops dramatically, to around 98°F (37°C), you can anticipate whelping within the next 12 hours. She will become increasingly restless and will eventually begin to strain with contractions.

The puppies are preceded by a water bag; after it has burst, the first puppy should be born soon. If a puppy appears stuck, you can use a washcloth and gently pull it downward (between the mother's hind legs) in time with her contractions. Never pull a puppy by a limb, tail, or head, though. You may wish to help the mother clear the puppy's face so that it can breathe, and you may wish to tie off the umbilical cord. Do this by tying dental floss around the cord about ¾ inch (around 2 centimeters) from the puppy, and then cutting the cord on the side away from the puppy. Make sure that for every puppy that comes out, a placenta comes out, too. Allow the dam to eat one placenta if she wants, as they contain important hormones, but they contribute to diarrhea, and one is enough.

Anything that might be an emergency in a large breed, is an emergency in a tiny breed. Err on the side of caution. You may have a whelping emergency if
• she has a dark green, black, or bloody discharge before the whelping date.
• more than 24 hours have passed since her temperature dropped without the onset of contractions.

• more than 2 hours of intermittent contractions have passed without progressing to hard, forceful contractions.
• more than 30 minutes of strong contractions have passed without producing a puppy.
• more than 15 minutes have passed since part of a puppy protruded through the vulva and the puppy makes no progress.
• large amounts of blood are passed during whelping.

Postnatal Care of the Dam

You must be especially vigilant not only with Yorkie puppies but with Yorkie dams as well. A post-whelping exam is advisable to ensure that all puppies and their placenta have been expelled. Sometimes a dead puppy is retained, causing a serious infection that often necessitates spaying.

Mastitis: You should be checking the dam's mammary glands throughout nursing for signs of mastitis, which includes pain, bloody discharge, and hard swelling. Home care includes hot compresses and gentle expression of the affected gland, while preventing puppies from nursing from it. Call your veterinarian for advice; antibiotics may be necessary.

Eclampsia: One of the greatest dangers to Yorkshire Terrier dams is the threat of eclampsia. It occurs when the amount of calcium lost in

A mother's love...

the milk is greater than the amount the body can absorb or produce. Eclampsia occurs most often during the first month of nursing but can also occur in late pregnancy. Small dogs, especially those with large litters that need a lot of milk, are predisposed.

Poor nutrition and improper supplementation can also contribute to the development of eclampsia. The optimal nutrition for the dam during the last half of her pregnancy and during nursing is a commercial puppy food. Because eclampsia occurs from too little calcium, many breeders try to avoid it by supplementing the dam with calcium during her pregnancy. However, this practice should be avoided because the excess calcium intake tends to decrease the body's efficiency in absorbing calcium from the diet and in mobilizing calcium from the bones—actually making eclampsia more likely. Supplementing with calcium during the first month of nursing, on the other hand, may be beneficial. You should discuss any supplementation with your veterinarian before implementing it, however.

Early signs of eclampsia include irritability, neglect of puppies, and restlessness, followed by salivation, facial itching, stiffness, fever, increased heart rate, and loss of balance. Final

"Hello, world!"

signs are severe muscle contractions and seizures. Eclampsia is a medical emergency that needs immediate treatment if the dam is to survive. Emergency treatment involves slow intravenous administration of calcium; following this, the puppies should be weaned as quickly as possible.

Neonatal Care

Newborns should have a regular respiration rhythm, a heart rate of more than 200 beats per minute, bright red gums, and a body temperature of 94 to 96°F. Yorkie birth weights range from about 2 ounces to 9 ounces, with 3 to 5 ounces being most common. Those under 3 ounces will need extra care in order to survive; those under 2 ounces seldom make it. Birth weight does not correlate with adult weight.

Monitor the puppies to make sure that they are getting milk; puppies with cleft palates will have milk bubbling out of their nostrils as they nurse. During normal development, the two sides of the roof of the mouth grow together and fuse before birth, but in some pups they fail to do so. This leaves an opening between the oral and nasal cavities, creating a number of problems; however, it can often be corrected surgically. Both genetic and environmental factors probably play a role; some breeders claim that prenatal administration of folic acid lowers the incidence.

Weigh each puppy on a gram scale daily. Although puppies will likely experience a slight drop in weight the first day, after that they should steadily gain weight, doubling their weight by 7 to 10 days of age. Most average-sized puppies will gain around 4 to 7 grams a day during the first few weeks.

Puppies can't regulate their body temperatures, and chilling can kill them. Maintain the temperature in part of the whelping box at about 85°F for the first week, 80°F for the second week, and 75°F for the third and fourth weeks. Overheating and dehydration can also have just as devastating effects, so make sure the puppies can crawl away from the heat. Never feed a chilled puppy.

Canine herpes: Some neonates die for no apparent reason. Probably some of these are victims of canine herpes. Affected puppies cry piteously and will not nurse. The herpes virus cannot replicate in high temperatures, and some puppies have been saved by placing them in incubators at the first sign of symptoms. If you suspect canine herpes, keep your puppies very warm and consult your veterinarian immediately.

Hand rearing: Abnormally small puppies or puppies that lose weight may need supplemental feedings. If the dam has eclampsia or mastitis, or is ignoring the puppies, you will also probably need to supplement. It's usually easier to tube-feed a newborn Yorkie than it is to bottle-feed one, but you will need your veterinarian to show you exactly how to do this. If you have a puppy that will nurse from a bottle, you should use the bottle so that the puppy's sucking instincts are satisfied. The puppies should be fed every 2 hours for the first week or so of life, slacking off to every 3 hours after the puppy has doubled its birth weight. The puppy must be stimulated to urinate and defecate after each feeding.

Small Talk
Hernias

Umbilical hernias, in which the opening around the umbilical cord fails to close properly, are a common occurrence in dogs. Inguinal hernias, which are noticeable as a swelling in the groin area, are a fairly common problem in Yorkshire Terriers. Most hernias are small and eventually only trap a small pocket of fat. Hernias in which the abdominal contents can be pushed out can pose the threat of eventually trapping and strangulating their contents and should be corrected surgically.

This is done by rubbing the urogenital area and anus with a warm damp cloth, simulating licking by the dam.

Tail Docking and Dewclaw Removal

If you plan to remove dewclaws and dock tails, it should be done within the first 5 days. After that time, it is usually best to leave them as nature intended or to wait until the puppy is older and can undergo anesthesia. Some disagreement exists on whether front dewclaws should be removed, but many breeders believe that it prevents painful injuries later in life. Rear dewclaws, if present, should be removed. Tail docking is even more controversial. Different countries differ in their views on tail docking. In the United States, it is customary to dock the tail so that about one third of its original length remains. That means leaving about ½ inch in a newborn puppy. If you have no intention of showing your Yorkie in conformation, or of selling to somebody who might care about tail length, there is no need to dock tails. A long tail is the norm in several European countries, and it does not interfere with any aspect of Yorkie well-being. In fact, tail docking is illegal in many countries because it is not without pain and stress to the puppy.

Growing Up Yorkie

Yorkie puppies should be born black with small tan markings. The nose can be lighter or pink spotted at birth. It will gradually turn darker in a few days. The puppies' eyes will begin to open at around 10 days of age, and

Small Talk
Testicle Descent

A fairly common defect of dogs is the failure of one or both testicles to descend normally into the scrotum. It's usually difficult to feel them in any puppy until a couple of weeks of age, but by 8 weeks you should be able to feel tiny testicles in a male's scrotum. Most are descended by 12 weeks, but some Yorkies have been known to have very late descending testicles. After the age of 4 months, the chances of testicles descending are quite low.

the ears, at around 2 weeks. Around this time they will also start attempting to walk. Be sure to give them solid footing—not slippery newspaper!

Weaning: Introduce hungry puppies to pureed food when they are about 3 weeks old. Do this when they are hungry. You may have to put a bit on their noses to get their tongues working and convince them this new substance is tasty. Some dogs catch on more quickly than others; don't worry if yours take a little longer. By about 4 to 6 weeks of age, the dam will begin weaning them herself, and the puppies will start to prefer solid foods.

Socialization: Few times are as fun as when the puppies first venture out of the whelping box and begin to explore the world. Your job now is to make sure that they are gradually exposed to new experiences without being exposed to danger or disease.

You want your puppies to meet new people, but too often people carry with them communicable diseases. Never allow anyone into your home who has come from a place where dogs have gathered, such as a dog show or animal shelter, unless they, at the very least, remove their shoes and refrain from handling the puppies. Although you may seem like a less than perfect host, your puppies' lives are too precious to take any chances. See pages 29–30 for a review of vaccinations and deworming.

The world ahead: Most reputable Yorkie breeders prefer that their puppies stay with them until they are at

Six-week old Yorkie puppies.

least 12 weeks of age, with tinier puppies staying home even longer. Your puppies should be leash trained and crate trained before they go to new homes. They should have spent time away from their littermates, had some car-riding experience, and met men, women, and children. They should have stolen your heart in the process. If they haven't, you shouldn't be breeding.

Good breeders worry. They worry that the people who desperately want a puppy today will tire of it tomorrow. They worry that the cozy bedroom described to them is really a pen in the garage. They worry that the motivations are not what they seem to be. Too many breeders have been burned by mistakenly placing their faith in people who seemed ideal. You need to listen with a cautious ear to what you are told, watch carefully how the entire family interacts with your dogs, and ask many questions. Your puppies are depending on you to weed out homes that could become living nightmares; they are depending on you for the rest of their lives.

When you finally find a home worthy of your puppy, the hardest part of breeding a litter still awaits: saying good-bye to the puppies you've grown to love. If you're a good breeder, you'll keep in touch with their new families throughout their lives. You'll be there to answer questions, act as a safety net, hear of the latest antics, and commiserate as they grow old. If you're a good breeder, you'll be rewarded by the lives your puppies have brightened, and you'll have created an extended family of Yorkie lovers.

Chapter Eleven

Yorkies Through the Years

When we welcome a Yorkie into our homes and hearts, we tend to dwell on the fun and excitement of puppyhood, and perhaps the satisfaction and companionship of adulthood. But too often we neglect to consider the special needs and joys of the senior Yorkie.

Old age is something to celebrate. It means that you've given your dog good care, that you've both enjoyed some good luck, and that you've had the privilege of sharing a full lifetime of your dog's companionship. Toy dogs, including Yorkshire Terriers, live long lives compared to larger dogs. But they still live short lives compared to ours.

Many people have unrealistic expectations about life expectancy for their dog, based upon the publicity given to unusually long-lived individuals. All dogs age at different rates, but by 10 or 11 years of age most Yorkshire Terriers are showing some definite signs of old age. Even so, they continue to age slowly, and most Yorkshire Terriers can live into their teens. Although the average life span is around 13 to 15 years, it's not uncommon to hear of a Yorkshire Terrier living into its late teens, and occasional rare individuals even reach into their twenties.

The first signs of aging often sneak up on you. One day you'll notice your perpetual puppy has finally calmed down, and on closer inspection you may realize his face has silvered and gait has stiffened. However young at heart, at some point your Yorkshire Terrier will begin to feel the effects of age, and you will need to know how to best help him cope.

Aging Gracefully

Yorkies have Peter Pan attitudes. They are perpetual puppies, ready to play their way into old age. This young at heart outlook helps keep your Yorkie young in body, but you must do your part to make his later years the best ones possible.

Older dogs tend to like a simpler life. A nap in the sun, a short car trip, a tasty meal, a few laps around the house, a leisurely stroll around the block, and a chance to snuggle may be enough to make an older dog's day complete.

Travel or boarding can be stressful for an older dog. Consider having a responsible house sitter stay with your dog if you must leave him. The house sitter should be familiar with your dog and any health problems he may have and should be well versed in Yorkie health and safety concerns.

Your Yorkshire Terrier may not be able to jump onto or off beds or chairs like he used to, either because of arthritis, general weakness, or visual problems. Try to arrange some steps or platforms that can help your dog reach the places he has enjoyed all his life.

Older Yorkies may be more susceptible to chilling in cold weather. They should wear a sweater if they go outside in the cold and have access to a warm, soft bed inside.

Some older Yorkshire Terriers become cranky and impatient, especially when dealing with puppies or boisterous children. Don't just excuse such behavioral changes, especially if sudden, simply as the result of aging. They could be symptoms of pain or illness.

Sensory loss: Older dogs may experience hearing or visual loss. The slight haziness that appears in the older dog's pupils is normal and has minimal effect upon vision, but some dogs may develop cataracts. These can be seen as almost white through the dog's pupils. Just as with people, severe cataracts can be removed and replaced with an artificial lens.

A long life comes from good care, good genes, and good luck.

Yorkies with vision loss can cope well as long as they are kept in familiar surroundings, and extra safety precautions are followed. For example, block open stairways or pools, don't move furniture, and place sound or scent beacons throughout the house or yard to help the dog locate specific landmarks. Lay pathways, such as gravel or block walkways outdoors and carpet runners indoors.

Yorkies with hearing loss can learn hand gestures and also respond to vibrations. It's never too late to teach an old dog new tricks.

Feeding: Keeping an older dog in ideal weight can be a difficult challenge. Both physical activity and

A Yorkie in his autumn years requires more diligent health monitoring.

metabolic rates decrease in older animals, so they require fewer calories to maintain the same weight. Excessive weight can place an added burden on the heart and the joints. However, very old dogs often tend to lose weight, which can be equally bad. Your dog needs a little cushion of fat so that she has something to fall back on if she gets sick.

Most older dogs do not require a special diet unless they have a particular medical need for it (see page 58). High-quality protein is especially important for healthy older dogs.

Older dogs should be fed several small meals and should be fed on time. Moistening dry food or feeding canned food can help a dog with dental problems enjoy his meal. Dogs with arthritis, especially affecting the neck, may find it more comfortable to eat elevated food or to eat while lying down.

Grooming: Older dogs can develop dry, itchy skin. Regular brushing can help by stimulating oil production. Older dogs tend to have a stronger body odor, but don't just ignore increased odors. They could indicate specific problems, such as periodontal disease, impacted anal sacs, seborrhea, ear infections, or even kidney disease. Older dogs may be more sensitive to having their hair pulled, and extensive grooming sessions can be taxing. If you've not already done so, your older Yorkie may find a closer clip refreshing, and you'll find it easier to care for. It's a good idea to learn to clip your dog yourself if she finds a day at the groomer's too taxing.

Periodontal disease is extremely common in older Yorkshire Terriers. The dog may have bad breath, lick his lips constantly, be reluctant to chew, or even have swelling around the mouth. A thorough tooth cleaning, possibly combined with drug therapy, is necessary to relieve these dogs' discomfort.

Senior Health

The older Yorkshire Terrier should have a checkup at least twice a year. Blood tests can detect early stages

Take time to smell the flowers.

of treatable diseases. Although older dogs present a somewhat greater anesthesia risk, a complete medical workup before anesthesia can be helpful in evaluating your dog's anesthesia risk.

Arthritis: Older dogs often suffer from arthritis, which causes intermittent inflammation, decreased range of motion, and pain. In some dogs, there is no obvious cause. In others, abnormal stresses or trauma to the joint can cause degeneration of the joint cartilage and underlying bone.

Conservative treatment entails keeping the dog's weight down, providing a soft warm bed, attending to injuries, and maintaining a program of exercise. Low-impact exercise such as walking every other day is best for dogs with signs of arthritis. Newer drugs, such as carprofen, are available from your veterinarian and may help alleviate some arthritic signs, but

Yorkies in their golden years enjoy a warm place from which to rule their households.

they should be used only with careful veterinary supervision. Some newer drugs and supplements may actually improve the joint. Polysulfated glycosaminoglycan increases the compressive resilience of cartilage. Glucosamine stimulates the synthesis of collagen and may help rejuvenate cartilage to some extent. Chondroitin sulfate helps to shield cartilage from destructive enzymes.

Illness: Older dogs may have less-efficient immune systems, making it increasingly important to shield them from infectious disease, chilling, overheating, and stress. At the same time, an older dog that is never exposed to other dogs may not need to be vaccinated as often or for as many diseases as a younger dog. This is an area of current controversy that you should discuss with your veterinarian.

An older Yorkie cannot tolerate the dehydration that results from continued vomiting or diarrhea, so you should never let it continue unchecked. Vomiting and diarrhea in an old dog can signal many different problems, some of which can be serious. In general, any ailment that an older dog has is magnified in severity compared to the same problems in a younger dog.

Dogs suffer from many of the same diseases of old age that humans do. Cancer accounts for almost half of all deaths in dogs over 10 years of age. Some signs of cancer are abnormal swellings that don't go away or that continue to grow, loss of appetite or difficulty eating or swallowing, weight loss, persistent lameness, bleeding, or difficulty breathing, urinating, or defecating. Most of these symptoms could also be associated with other disorders so that only a veterinary examination can determine the real problem.

Hyperadrenocorticism (Cushing's syndrome) is typically seen in middle-aged or older dogs, and Yorkies are one of the breeds in which it's most often seen. It results when the body produces too much of the hormone cortisol, most often because of a non-malignant tumor on the pituitary gland in the brain, or less often, a tumor on the adrenal glands. The overstimulation with cortisol produces a variety of signs including increased hunger, thirst, and urination, as well as hair loss, muscle atrophy, lack of energy, and a pot-bellied appearance.

Several screening tests are available. A normal urine cortisol-to-creatinine ratio usually indicates that a dog doesn't have hyperadrenocorticism; an abnormal ACTH stimulation test suggests the dog does have it. Treatment is usually with drugs, which must be continued throughout the dog's life.

Although a hereditary mechanism has not been identified, the prevalence of hyperadrenocorticism in some breeds suggests a genetic component in at least these breeds. Affected Yorkies should not be bred.

When You've Done Everything

If you are lucky enough to have a Yorkshire Terrier senior, you still must accept that your time together is all the more precious and ultimately will end. Heart disease, kidney failure, and

Small Talk
Symptoms and Some of Their Possible Causes in Older Dogs
- Diarrhea: kidney or liver disease, pancreatitis
- Coughing: heart disease, tracheal collapse, lung cancer
- Difficulty eating: periodontal disease, oral tumors
- Decreased appetite: kidney, liver, or heart disease; pancreatitis; cancer
- Increased appetite: diabetes, Cushing's syndrome
- Weight loss: heart, liver, or kidney disease; diabetes; cancer
- Abdominal distention: heart or kidney disease, Cushing's Syndrome, tumor
- Increased urination: diabetes, kidney or liver disease, cystitis, Cushing's syndrome
- Limping: arthritis, patellar luxation
- Nasal discharge: tumor, periodontal disease

Cherish your time together, just as you always have.

cancer eventually claim most of these seniors. Early detection can help delay their effects but, unfortunately, can seldom prevent them ultimately.

Yorkshire Terriers play the roles of child, confidant, and best friend. They are the single most important being in many peoples' lives. Sometimes it seems like it would be easier if they were just dogs—but they're not. Grief is the ultimate price that must be paid for love; it is a high price, but the years you have shared with your Yorkshire Terrier truly are priceless.

Grief: Coming to terms with losing a dog who is so vital to your happiness is one of the most difficult challenges many people will ever face. Yet one day you will have to meet that sad challenge. Denial is the first reaction you may have to the news your dog has a terminal illness. It's a natural reaction that protects us from the emotional impact of the painful truth. It also goads many people into seeking a second opinion and exploring every possibility for curing their friend. Often, as it becomes clear nothing can help, the next reaction is anger—anger that dogs live so short a time, anger that the treatments for humans are not available to dogs, and even anger at those who have older dogs. Anger eventually becomes depression, when the truth is accepted and the futility of fighting acknowledged. Depression can begin well before actually losing a dog, and last well after. It can involve such a feeling of helplessness and defeat that a person may not even try some reasonable therapies for their dog. Although depression is natural, protracted depression can be extremely damaging. Pet bereavement counselors are available at many veterinary schools.

The last stage of grief is acceptance. Accepting the loss of a loved one doesn't mean that you don't care; it just means that you realize that you have to do so in order to continue living and loving again. In deciding what is best for you and your dog, and in getting through this terribly difficult part of your life, consider how your own stage of grieving my be affecting your decisions. Your veterinarian should be able to give you a more objective view of what your options are.

Euthanasia: Many terminal illnesses make your dog feel very ill, and there comes a point where your desire to keep your friend with you as long as possible may not be the kindest thing for either of you. If your dog consistently declines to eat, even treats, this is usually a sign that he doesn't feel well, and a signal that you must begin to face the prospect of doing what is best for your beloved friend.

Euthanasia is a difficult and personal decision that no one wants to make. Consider if your dog has a reasonable chance of getting better, and how your dog seems to feel. Ask yourself if your dog is getting pleasure out of life, and if he enjoys most of his days. Financial considerations can be a factor if it means going into debt in exchange for just a little more time together. Your own emotional state must also be considered. For every person the ultimate point is different. Most people probably put off doing something for longer than is really the kindest thing because they don't want to act in haste and be haunted by thoughts that just maybe it was a temporary setback. And, of course, they put it off because they can't stand the thought.

We all wish that if our dog has to go, he would fall asleep and never wake up. This, unfortunately, seldom happens. Even when it does, you are left with the regret that you never got to say goodbye. The closest you

Forever in your heart...

can come to this is with euthanasia. Euthanasia is painless and involves giving an overdose of an anesthetic. Essentially the dog will fall asleep and die almost instantly. In a very sick dog, because the circulation

Small Talk
In Loving Memory

One of the noblest tributes to a cherished Yorkshire Terrier is to donate in his or her memory to Yorkshire Terrier Rescue or to health research through the YTCA Foundation or the AKC Canine Health Foundation (see page 148).

Sometimes it seems it would be easier if they were just dogs—but Yorkies often play the roles of child and best friend; losing one can be no less difficult.

". . . the only worse loss would be never sharing it again."

may be compromised, this may take slightly longer, but the dog is not conscious.

If you do decide that euthanasia is the kindest farewell gesture for your beloved friend, discuss with your veterinarian beforehand what will happen. You may ask about giving your dog a tranquilizer beforehand, or having the doctor meet you at home. Although it won't be easy, try to remain with your dog so that his last moments will be filled with your love. Try to recall the wonderful times you have shared and realize that however painful losing such a once-in-a-lifetime friend is, it is better than never having had such a partner at all.

After losing such a cherished friend, many people say they will never expose themselves to that kind of pain by loving another dog. Some also see giving their love to another dog as being unfaithful to the first. No dog will ever take the place of your departed dog, and the love you had for your first dog will not be lessened by loving another. If you had so much to give and share with one dog, the only worse loss would be never sharing it again. Why not let a cold nose warm your heart and your lap once again?

Chapter Twelve

The Yorkshire Terrier Standard of Perfection

General Appearance

That of a long-haired toy terrier whose blue and tan coat is parted on the face and from the base of the skull to the end of the tail and hangs evenly and quite straight down each side of body. The body is neat, compact and well proportioned. The dog's high head carriage and confident manner should give the appearance of vigor and self-importance.

Head

Small and rather flat on top, the *skull* not too prominent or round, the *muzzle* not too long, with the *bite*

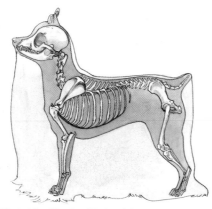

Yorkshire Terrier Skeletal Anatomy.

neither undershot nor overshot and teeth sound. Either scissors bite or level bite is acceptable. The *nose* is black. *Eyes* are medium in size and not too prominent; dark in color and sparkling with a sharp, intelligent expression. Eye rims are dark. Ears are small, V-shaped, carried erect, and set not too far apart.

Body

Well proportioned and very compact. The back is rather short, the back line level, with height at shoulder the same as at the rump.

Legs and Feet

Forelegs should be straight, elbows neither in nor out. *Hind legs* straight when viewed from behind, but stifles are moderately bent when viewed from the sides. *Feet* are round with black toenails. Dewclaws, if any, are generally removed from the hind legs. Dewclaws on the forelegs may be removed.

Tail

Docked to a medium length and carried slightly higher than the level of the back.

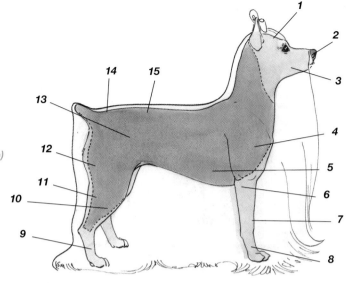

1. Skull
2. Nose
3. Muzzle
4. Shoulder
5. Chest
6. Elbow
7. Forearm
8. Pastern
9. Hock
10. Stifle
11. Lower Thigh
12. Upper Thigh
13. Loin
14. Rump (Croup)
15. Back

External anatomy of the Yorkshire Terrier, showing areas from which the tan and blue coat grows.

Coat

Quality, texture and quantity of coat are of prime importance. Hair is glossy, fine and silky in texture. Coat on the body is moderately long and perfectly straight (not wavy). It may be trimmed to floor length to give ease of movement and a neater appearance, if desired. The fall on the head is long, tied with one bow in center of head or parted in the middle and tied with two bows. Hair on muzzle is very long. Hair should be trimmed short on tips of ears and may be trimmed on feet to give them a neat appearance.

Colors

Puppies are born black and tan and are normally darker in body color, showing an intermingling of black hair in the tan until they are matured. Color of hair on body and richness of tan on head and legs are of prime importance in adult dogs, to which the following color requirements apply: Blue: Is a dark steel-blue, not a silver-blue and not mingled with fawn, bronzy, or black hairs. Tan: All tan hair is darker at the roots than in the middle, shading to still lighter tan at the tips. There should be no sooty or black hair intermingled with any of the tan.

Color on Body

The blue extends over the body from back of neck to root of tail. Hair on tail is a darker blue, especially at end of tail.

"A long-haired toy terrier…"

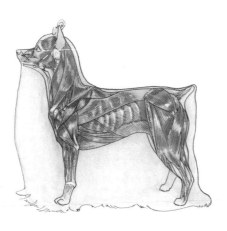

Yorkshire Terrier musculature.

Headfall

A rich golden tan, deeper in color at sides of head, at ear roots and on the muzzle, with ears a deep rich tan. Tan color should not extend down on back of neck.

Chest and Legs

A bright, rich tan, not extending above the elbow on the forelegs nor above the stifle on the hind legs.

Weight

Must not exceed seven pounds.

Approved April 12, 1966

Yorkie Resources

Organizations

Yorkshire Terrier Club of America
(YCTA)
Shirley A. Patterson, Secretary
P.O. Box 271
St. Peters, PA 19470-0271
www.ytca.org

YTCA Foundation
Robert Franzoni, Treasurer
8062 Cannonball Gate Road
Warrenton, VA 20186
*http://members.aol.com/
GoldenFern/YorkshireTerrier
Foundation.htm*

Canadian Yorkshire Terrier
Association
Edie Ovens, Secretary
16152 Hurontario Street
Caledon, Ontario L0N 1C0
(905) 838-4178
E-mail: yorkies@ica.net

The Yorkshire Terrier Club (UK)
Mrs Hazel Hammersley
4, Stookes Way
Yateley, Hampshire GU46 6YY
UK
Tel: 01252 871238
http://www.ytc.org.uk/

Yorkshire Terrier Club of New South
Wales
Mrs Marie Watt, Secretary
1433 The Northern Road
Bringelly NSW 2171
Australia

Other National Clubs

American Kennel Club (AKC)
5580 Centerview Drive
Raleigh, NC 27606-3390
(919) 233-9767
E-mail: info@akc.org
http://www.akc.org/

Canadian Kennel Club (CKC)
89 Skyway Avenue, Suite 100
Etobicoke, Ontario M9W 6R4
(800) 250-8040
E-mail: information@ckc.ca
http://www.ckc.ca/

United Kennel Club (UKC)
100 East Kilgore Road
Kalamazoo, MI 49001-5593
(616) 343-9020
http://www.ukcdogs.com/

Other National All-breed Kennel
  Clubs
*http://henceforths.com/kennel_
  clubs.htm*

Canine Eye Registration Foundation
  (CERF)
1248 Lynn Hall, Purdue University
West Lafayette, IN 47907
(765) 494-8179
*http://www.vet.purdue.edu:80/
  ~yshen/cerf.html*

AKC Canine Health Foundation
www.akcchf.org

Orthopedic Foundation for Animals
  (OFA)
2300 E. Nifong Boulevard
Columbia, MO 65201
(573) 442-0418
http://www.offa.org/

Home Again Microchip Service
1-800-LONELY-ONE

Therapy Dogs International
88 Bartley Road
Flanders, NJ 07836
(973) 252-9800
http://www.tdi-dog.org/

Periodicals
Top Notch Toys Magazine
Doll-McGinnis Enterprises
8848 Beverly Hills
Lakeland, FL 33809
(813) 858-3839
*http://www.dmcg.com/pubs/
  topnotchtoys/tnt_index.html*

The Yorkshire Terrier Annual
www.hoflin.com

Yorkshire Terrier Journal (German)
www.yorkshire-terrier-journal.com

AKC Gazette
*http://www.akc.org/insideAKC/
  resources/subs.cfm*

Rescue
Canadian Yorkshire Terrier Rescue: *http://can_yorkshire_rescue.tripod.
  com/*
Save Our Small Dogs: *http://www.petfinder.org/shelters/sosdogs.html*
United Yorkie Rescue: *http://www.unitedyorkierescue.org/*
Yorkie Rescue Homepage: *http://www.angelfire.com/in2/yorkies/*
Yorkshire Terrier National Rescue: *www.yorkshireterrierrescue.com*
Yorkshire Terrier Rescue Groups: *www.netpets.com/dogs/dogresc/breeds/
  dogyork.html*
Yorkshire Terrier Rescue Network: *www.yorkshireterrierrescue.net*
YTCA Rescue: *http://www.ytca.org/rescue.html*

Dog World Magazine
www.dogworldmag.com

Dog Fancy Magazine
www.dogfancy.com

Yorkshire Terriers (Popular Dogs
    Series)
www.animalnetwork.com

Books

Brearley, Joan McDonald. *Book of the Yorkshire Terrier*. Neptune City, NJ: TFH, 1984.

Coile, D. Caroline. *Show Me! A Dog Showing Primer*. Hauppauge, NY: Barron's Educational Series, Inc., 1997.

——. *Encyclopedia of Dog Breeds*. Hauppauge, NY: Barron's Educational Series, Inc., 1998.

——. *Beyond Fetch: Fun Interactive Activities for You and Your Dog*. New York: Wiley, 2003.

Gewirtz, Elaine. *Your Yorkshire Terrier's Life*. Roseville, CA: Prima, 2000.

Gordon, Joan. *The New Complete Yorkshire Terrier*. New York: Howell, 1993.

Haynes, Richard. *Living With a Yorkshire Terrier*. Hauppauge, NY: Barron's Educational Series, Inc., 2003.

Jackson, Janet. *A New Owner's Guide to Yorkshire Terriers*. Neptune City, NJ: TFH, 1996.

Kriechbaumer, Armin. *Yorkshire Terriers: Everything About Purchase, Care, Nutrition, Breeding, Behavior, and Training.*
Hauppauge, NY: Barron's Educational Series, Inc., 1996.

Lemire, Sandra. *Yorkies Head to Tail*. New Orleans, LA: Paper Chase, 1999.

Linzy, Jan. *Yorkshire Terrier Champions, 1984–2001*. Incline Village, NV: Camino Books, 2003.

Palika, Liz. *Complete Idiot's Guide to Yorkshire Terriers*. Alpha, 2003.

Videos

AKC Breed Standard Video
www.akc.org/store/
(919) 233-9767

International Videos
http://www.sweetyblue.com/Sweety/
    Principali/Nkc.html#

AMP Grooming the Yorkshire Terrier
http://www.4mdogbooks.com/
    H-GRM.HTML

Web Pages

International Yorkie News
http://www.henceforths.com

Yorkie Club
http://www.yorkyclub.com/

Sweety Blue
http://www.sweetyblue.com

Yorkshire Terrier Top Sites
*http://www.topsitelists.com/start/
    yorkie/*

Anima (search site for Yorkshire
    Terrier Convention)
www.anima.com

Working Yorkies
*http://www.geocities.com/
    workingyorkie/*

Yorkshire Terrier Journal
www.yorkshire-terrier-journal.com

Yorkie Portal
http://www.yorkie.at/index.php

Norsk Yorkshire Terrier Web
http://members.tripod.com/ytnytt/

Judging the Yorkshire Terrier
*http://www.geocities.com/~dugmore/
    seminar.html*
*http://www.worldclassdogs.com/
    YBTJ/YBTJ_314_Main.html*
http://www.ytca.org/education1.html

AKC Canine Health Foundation
*http://www.akcchf.org/new_pages/
    News/News_Nav.htm*

Animal CPR
*http://members.aol.com/
    henryhbk/acpr.html*

Doggy.com
www.doggy.com

The Dog Agility Page
http://www.dogpatch.org/agility/

The Dog Obedience and Training
    Page
http://www.dogpatch.org/obed/

Dr. P's Dog Training Links
*http://www.uwsp.edu/acad/psych/
    dog/dog.htm*

Pet Groomer
www.petgroomer.com

Infodog Dog Show Site
http://www.infodog.com/main.htm

National Animal Poison Control
    Center
(800) 548-2423
http://www.napcc.aspca.org/

Index

age 15–16
aggression 48–50
agility trials 10, 12, 115–118
allergies
  flea 78–79
  food 58–59
American Kennel Club 5, 16, 75,
  110, 113, 115–116, 123, 147
anal sacs 89
anatomy
  external 145
  internal 53
  musculature 146
  skeletal 144
antifreeze poisoning 106
appetite loss 87
arthritis 137–138
artificial respiration 102

barking 48
bathing 68–70
behavior problems 43–50
biting 48–50
bleeding
  first aid for 104
  prolonged 101–102
blood tests 100
body language 44
breeders 12–15, 17
breeding 10, 12, 123–133
brushing 62–64

caesarean 17, 127
calcium supplementation 129
Canine Good Citizen 112,
  114–115
cardiopulmonary resuscitation
  103
cataracts 101, 135
cats (and Yorkies) 8, 29
celebrity owners 6
children (and Yorkies) 9, 10, 26
chocolate 107

choosing 10–18
clicker training 37–38
clubs 5, 147
coat 11, 145
coat care 7–8, 61–79
collar 20–21, 22
color 11, 13, 145–146
come command 39–40
conformation 12, 26–28,
  108–110, 144–146
coprophagia 56
corneal dystrophy 100–101
coughing 89–91
crate 21–23, 24
Cushing's syndrome 56–57,
  100, 139

dangers 19–20, 105–107, 118
dehydration 19, 138
dental care 82–84

dental occlusion 83
destructive behavior 46–47
dewclaws 18
diabetes 56–57, 59, 93
diarrhea 88, 106, 107, 138, 139
diets 52–55
disc catching 119–120
dog shows 3–5, 14, 108–110
dogs (other, and Yorkies) 26–28
doll faced 13
down command 41
dry eye 99–100
drying 70–71

ears
  care 84–85
  conformation 144
  cropped 3
  taping 34
  trimming 65

earthdog 121
eclampsia 128–130
equipment 22, 36, 62, 102
euthanasia 141–143
exercise 9, 46, 137
eyes
  conformation 144
  disorders 98–101

fearfulness 47–48, 49
fence 23
fever 87
fighting 8, 27–28
first aid 102–106
fleas 79
flyball 120–121
fontanel 16, 98
food
  commercial 53–54
  puppy 32–33
  raw 52–54
  training rewards 35–36
fractures 105

grief 140
grooming 61–77
  geriatric 136
  professional 76–77
  puppy 33–34
  supplies 62
growth, stunted, 97
gum color 86

hair types 70
hair, growing 72
hand rearing 131
harness 21, 22
health concerns 11
heart disease 56–57, 60, 92, 139
heartworms 31
heat stroke 102
heel command 41–42
hernias 131
herpes 131
history 1–6
housetraining 23–25, 45–47
Huddersfield Ben 3, 4

hunting 1–2
hydrocephalus 10, 97–98
hypoglycemia 10, 32–33, 54, 103
hypoplasia of dens 96
hypothermia 102–103
hypothyroidism 56–57, 102

identification 21
inbreeding 125
international popularity 5

kidney disease 60, 92, 100, 139
kindergarten 26

leash 22
Legg-Calve'-Perthes disease 96
lethargy 87
lifespan 134
limited registration 16
limping 93–96
litterbox 24
liver disease 59, 100

mange 80–81
mastitis 128
mites 80–81
molera 10, 16

nail care 81–82
neonatal care 130–131
neutering 31–32
nutrition 51–52

obedience 10, 12
obedience trials 110–113
obesity 56–57
Orthopedic Foundation for
  Animals 11, 95, 148

pancreatitis 59–60
parasites
  external 79–81
  internal 30–31
patellar luxation 10, 94–96
patent ductus arteriosis 92
pedigree 5, 16, 125

personality 8
pet quality 13
poisoning 106–107
popularity 5–6, 123
portosystemic shunt 97
pregnancy 126–127
price 16–18
progressive retinal atrophy 101
pulse 87
puppies 18, 29–34, 130–133

rats (and Yorkies) 2, 8
registration papers 16
registrations 5–6, 123–133
rescues 15
reverse sneezing 91

safety 19–20, 105–107, 118
seizures 96–98, 102, 106, 107
separation anxiety 47
shaker syndrome 98
sit command 38
size 5, 9–10, 13, 22
skin problems 78–79

snake bite 105
socialization 25–26, 132
spaying 31–32
standard 10, 13, 108, 144–146
stings 105–106
swimming 21

tail docking 131–132
teacup Yorkies 10, 13
teeth 10, 82–84, 136
temperament 12
temperature 88, 103–104, 131
terrier breeds 2, 5
terrier roots 1, 2–3, 8, 26, 29,
    110
testicles 12, 132
therapy dogs 121–122
thunder, fear of 47–48
ticks 79–80
topknot 71–74, 114–115
toys 22
tracheal collapse 21, 41, 89,
    90–91
tracking 117–119

training equipment 36
tricks 42–43
trimming 64–68, 70

urinary stones 58, 59, 92–93
urination 45–46, 91–93

vaccinations 29–30, 138
vomiting 88, 106, 107, 138
von Willebrand's disease
    101–102

water 58
weaning 132
weight 130, 135–136, 139
weight loss 58
whelping 127–128
worms 30–31
wrapping 75

Yorkshire Terrier Club of
    America 5, 14, 147

x-pen 22–23